TOUGH LOVE

TOUGH LOVE

The Answer to Tackling Drug Addiction & Seeing Change
Copyright © 2016 Peter Lyndon-James

Apart from any fair dealing for the purposes of private study, research or criticism or review as permitted under the Copyright Act, no part of this book may be reproduced by any process without the written permission of the publisher.

Some names have been changed to protect the privacy of individuals.

Peter Lyndon-James
PO Box 1970, MIDLAND DC WA 6936
Email orders: peter@lyndonjames.com.au

ISBN: 978-0-646-96670-0 (paperback)
ISBN: 978-0-6453367-1-9 (ePub)

Scripture quotations marked (NIV) are taken from the Holy Bible, New International Version®, NIV®. Copyright © 1973, 1978, 1984, 2011 by Biblica, Inc.™ Used by permission of Zondervan. All rights reserved worldwide. www.zondervan.com The "NIV" and "New International Version" are trademarks registered in the United States Patent and Trademark Office by Biblica, Inc.™

Scripture quotations noted (NLT) are taken from the Holy Bible, New Living Translation, copyright ©1996, 2004, 2007, 2013, 2015 by Tyndale House Foundation. Used by permission of Tyndale House Publishers, Inc., Carol Stream, Illinois 60188. All rights reserved.

Scripture quotations noted (ESV) are from the ESV® Bible (The Holy Bible, English Standard Version®), copyright © 2001 by Crossway, a publishing ministry of Good News Publishers. Used by permission. All rights reserved.

Acknowledgements:
Steve Blizard for proofreading and editing this book. Jennifer Maly and Paper Lions Australia for assisting Steve.
Cover art and direction by Nik Gall - www.propellerbrands.com.au
Cover photography by Paul Allen, Lensflair - www.lensflair.net.au
Cover talent - Daniel Swain
Typesetting by Images on Paper (WA) Pty Ltd
10/64-66 Kent Street, Cannington WA 6107

Printing by Scott Print
4 Aberdeen Street, Perth WA 6000

processgreen™

CONTENTS

Introduction 5

Chapter 1 - My Background 11

Chapter 2 - The Work Of Shalom House 19

Chapter 3 - Understanding Ice 27

Chapter 4 - Coping With An Addict 65

Chapter 5 - Desperate Families 79

Chapter 6 - How To Get Your Loved One Back Again 95

Chapter 7 - Ten Questions From The Other Side 149

Chapter 8 - Shalom House Testimonies 199

Chapter 9 - You're Not Just A Fart In The Wind 229

Glossary 243

TOUGH LOVE

INTRODUCTION

I woke up one morning after a sixteen-day, no-sleep bender on the meth. At the time, I was selling $40,000 of meth on average every day as well as a large amount of firearms; 9mms, .44 Magnums, Colts, sawn-off shotguns, explosives and everything else that comes with that sort of life. You name it, I had it, I was a mess. My daily routine was to wake up, have a shot of meth, inject some steroids in my butt, smoke a few cones; then I was off to do business.

But not this time. I woke up to the sound of the coppers yelling "Get on the floor, hands behind your head, don't move."

My wife, Amanda, was naked with a towel around her, with our nine-month-old son, Rhyan, in her arms. There was a police helicopter over the top of the house. The Tactical Response Group had just come through the windows and the front door with shotguns in hand, donned with bulletproof vests and safety gear. Not a good way to wake up, but for me, it was the standard norm, this used to happen often. You can't do what I was doing and expect anything else.

> **"I hated who I was and what I stood for.
> I hated everything that I had become,
> but I didn't know how to change."**

I hated who I was and what I stood for. I hated everything that I had become, but I didn't know how to change. Every time I tried, I fell flat on my face.

I tried to change, to hang out with the geeks, do the normal stuff, but every time, I felt like I was a weed and that I did not belong. So, I went back to hanging around those people who I felt comfortable with, but the problem was they were doing things that I wanted to stop doing, and I would fall again. I moved from state to state, running from myself but wherever I went, I went. I was the problem; it was me and what was in me.

My whole life I wished I was a geek, a normal person living a normal life doing normal things. I went to sixteen schools and only ever really made Grade Six. I would have given anything as a child to be able to go to one school, to go on a family holiday with Mum and Dad, to run up the corridor in the mornings and jump into bed with them for a cuddle, but I never had any of that. I have never played normal sports, been on family holidays, or even had my parents attend anything that I ever did, except when they appeared at the Perth Children's Court to hand me over to the government to be made a ward of the state.

My life has done a 180-degree turnaround. I've been a geek now for about fifteen years. A geek to me, by the way, is a normal person, one who is a productive member of society, free from the influence of alcohol and other life-controlling substances. I have a saying that you may hear throughout this book: "You can take the prisoner out of prison, but then you have to get the prison out of the prisoner," and that's not an easy task.

I specialise in two things. The first is changing a person's life and the second is showing a person or family how to bring a person to the point of wanting to change. You can lead a horse to water, but you can't make it drink.

Many people want help for a person who does not want it or is never ready for it. I believe that you don't have to get it wrong to get it right and a wise man learns from those who have gone ahead. I've gone ahead, my life's changed and all I do is help others to break free from what held me captive for most of my life.

You may know a person caught up in addiction and are not sure what to do or how to help. In this book, I plan to equip you on how to help as well as protect yourself and your family as it all unfolds, so here we go.

The reason behind "Tough Love."

My name is Pete and I run a men's rehabilitation centre, Shalom House, located in the heart of the Swan Valley in Henley Brook, an outer suburb of Perth, Western Australia. Currently, we have residential capacity for 60 residents across nine properties. The main property consists of three houses that will accommodate 33 fellas; the second facility combines two houses for 20 fellas, and the other four premises are family-sized that can house three - five residents.

The purpose of this book is that in our community and nation, we have an epidemic on our hands. We have a unique drug on the streets now that's destroying families at a rate like no drug has ever done before. It not only binds a person up in addiction, but it changes them – the way they speak, the way they act and the way they treat those around them. This drug changes the most fun-loving family man into the most dishonest, deceitful, disrespectful, untrustworthy, manipulative person you will ever meet.

They lie, steal and cheat to get what they need or want. They are completely unpredictable and are not safe to be around or to be trusted. You should treat every word that comes out of their mouth as a lie. Yes, you guessed it, we're talking about a meth user, a crackhead, a junkie, a drug addict, a person bound up in addiction.

I constantly carry two mobile phones. These phones aren't used to sell drugs like I used to, but to deal with the volume of calls I get from people wanting help on behalf of a person caught up in addiction to drugs. Ninety percent of my calls are from people who are either suffering the effects of methamphetamines or are ringing on behalf of someone they know who is a user.

At Shalom House, we specialise in helping people break free from life-controlling issues such as meth and other drugs. We focus on bringing a person to the point where they want to change, where they are wanting to make the decision to turn their life around so badly that they will finally stop taking drugs. It is my intention to equip you and your family with strategies on how to successfully handle a person on drugs. Though this book will primarily focus on meth, the principles apply across the board for all forms of addiction. Hopefully, by the time you finish this book, you will have a much better idea of what to do and how to handle the challenges ahead.

TOUGH LOVE

CHAPTER
~1~

My Background

I grew up in prisons and institutions from the age of nine, having spent most of my childhood locked up or on the streets. I was what is widely referred to as being institutionalised. I would be locked up for six months and then out for a week, then back in for nine months, out for a month then back in for another six. I spent seven years off and on in Longmore Juvenile Detention Centre, two years in Riverbank Juvenile Detention Centre and then graduated to prison in 1991. Since then I have spent time in all the prisons in Perth, WA.

In 2001, when my life turned around, I was selling on average two and a half kilos of methamphetamines a day as well as a large amount of firearms and explosives. I've been sticking needles in my arms and using drugs for as long as I can remember. I often tell people that while I spent twenty-six years in and out of institutions and prisons from the age of nine, even when I wasn't in prison, I was still in prison.

I have a saying, "You can take the prisoner out of prison, but then you must get the prison out of the prisoner."

I remember the first time I smoked marijuana. I was ten years old, hanging out at a mate's house in a block of flats in the Perth CBD. I smoked my first cone and laid on the floor in the toilet for what felt like days, chucking what I call a "whitey". Blood drained from my face, and my skin went ghostly white while I was throwing my guts up in the dunny, but I still enjoyed the high that it gave me.

The first time I tried speed, I was at a house in Osborne Park. I had to shoot myself up as the other fella with me had to run to the toilet due to the effect that the drugs had on him. The feeling that it gave me was something that I would continually crave for many years to come. I felt like I was invincible and had more energy than I had ever had before. All of a sudden, life was exciting, and I felt I could do anything. I have tried every drug there is over the years: ecstasy, heroin, cocaine, LSD, ice and all types of benzos and other prescription drugs. You name it, I've had it, but my drug of choice has always been the meth or amphetamines.

I've been running from myself for most of my life. I would travel to Kalgoorlie, score a packet, work my way up to an eight ball, then get to an ounce. I could see that I was heading for jail, so I would run to another town and the cycle would continue. I moved from Kalgoorlie to Adelaide, from Adelaide to Sydney, from Sydney to Queensland and then from Queensland to

Perth. It seemed no matter how hard I tried, I couldn't break free from addiction. I've been around Australia at least seven times running from myself, but wherever I went, I went. I was the problem.

> **"When I was released from prison in 2001, after doing 12 months of a five-year sentence, I decided to sell drugs for a living. Within three months, I was selling an average of $40,000 per day of methamphetamines."**

It's not just as easy as saying stop using drugs even though people say it is; well it wasn't for me anyway. I had a whole lifetime of crap in me that was adding fuel to my stupid choices, plus I really liked drugs. I'm sad to say I still do, even though I don't use them anymore. When I was released from prison in 2001, after doing 12 months of a five-year sentence, I decided to sell drugs for a living.

Within three months, I was selling an average of $40,000 per day of methamphetamines. I used to drive around with two and a half kilos of the purest meth you could get your hands on under my seat. On the passenger's side floor, I had a whole collection of handguns. There were 9mm Glocks, .38 revolvers, a .44 Magnum revolver to name a few. I used to get brand new .22 pistols in the box, not to mention boxes of dynamite and C-4 explosives. You may think I'm kidding, but I'm not. I went big and bad quick, so quick that if you were to ask me how it happened, well, that I couldn't tell you, but I was there.

My drug use was that bad I used to go for sixteen days without sleep. I was sticking steroids in my butt and ice in my veins. I used to get off on giving people shots that would drop them to the floor screaming for hours. You name it, I've been through it. I've been stuck in a roof for two days thinking people were following me who weren't there. I've pulled people out of their cars because I thought that they were following me, but they weren't.

One time I sat for thirty-six hours in a little shed, with a camera pole that I made that went through the roof. At one stage, I was President of the Loopers Club. King Looper, they called me. I would sit there looking at the camera monitor for hours trying to find those who were following me, but in reality, I was suffering extreme psychosis.

I've been in a mental health ward and kept against my own free will as well as chained to a hospital bed because I had lost the plot. I've been raided by the police more times than I can remember. The Police Tactical Response Group wearing bulletproof vests busted my door down while holding shotguns many times as the police helicopter flew over the top of my home. You name it; I've done it. Right at the end, just before my life turned around, I was under surveillance like I'd never experienced in my life or ever thought was possible. They had people, resources and equipment that I never dreamed existed – well, only in the movies anyway.

My Wife

I've been with Amanda for 27 years and we have been married for 22 years. Amanda and I met in a pub in Kelmscott, a suburb of Perth, where I was selling drugs. Amanda came from Wongan Hills, a small country town in WA's Wheatbelt. She grew up normal, nothing like me, a complete opposite. She was from a good hardworking family, but tragically, I ruined many years of her life, taking her on an adventure that she would never forget. I have done everything a man should never do to his wife.

For a long time, I virtually destroyed her. Emotionally and mentally scarring her by my actions, never telling her what I was up to. I regret having been unfaithful to her more times than I can remember, leading her astray into a world that wasn't her own. The reason why I've shared this is not to glorify the world that I come from or the life that I have lived, but rather to try to paint a picture so that you can see that I have an idea of what I've written about in this book.

For my whole life, I really hated myself. I hated who I was and what I did. My life has now changed. Today, my marriage has never been stronger. I get the privilege to wake up next to my wife on a daily basis, knowing she still loves me and that she makes my heart flutter. I have broken free from what held me captive for many years and now I want to dedicate my life to helping other people do the same.

My family

Allow me to describe my family. They are the drug addict, the thief, the prostitute, the adulterer, the rejected and the despised. They are the people in society that people can't stand, who they turn from and look down upon. They are my brothers and my sisters; they are who I grew up with, who I care about and who I feel comfortable being around. A lot of us don't want to be who we are, but we don't know how to change and when we do try to hang around the geeks, the normal people, we feel like a weed, like we don't belong so we go back to where we feel comfortable. The problem is where we feel comfortable, everyone is doing what we don't want to do – we're trapped. Well, I've found a way out, and I want to show you how. Not only do I want to show you, but I want you to share this with others. I want to equip you to help others, not to go where I went, nor do what I've done or hurt people like I've hurt them.

I can't stand religion

This book is written in a manner that I trust is acceptable to all people, regardless of their beliefs or views about God. The last thing I want to do is push religion down your throat. More than likely, religious people will probably criticise me for not mentioning God as often as they would like. However, those people who have been scared away or put off by religion will probably thank me for it. Either way, please know that I don't want to do anything that hurts or disrespects my readers in any way, shape or form. No matter what your stance, I care about you.

It's really important to state from the start that I can't stand religion. I'm not a religious man, but I am a Christian, whom some would say holds to a form of religion. I try, to the best of my ability, to live what I believe and love God with all my heart. I often say that if the church of God was like Hungry Jacks, then it would be chockers, or full to the rafters, but it's not. It's splintered and broken up into many denominations, and this can be confusing to the average person.

Often a person can get hurt or scared by one group or denomination and ends up putting everyone else in the same group, unfortunately cutting them off from the message they need to hear. Some have had faith pushed down their throats and been forced to go to church. So as an adult they want nothing to do with it. Or they have had faith communicated to them by a person who did not live by what they were advocating, and they have said to themselves, "Well, if religion is like that, I want no part of it."

Please take comfort in the knowledge that the author desires that that the message of this book may be acceptable to all people, and respects your personal beliefs.

TOUGH LOVE

CHAPTER ~2~

The Work Of Shalom House

In July 2012, I started Shalom House. We have the reputation of being the strictest rehabilitation centre in Australia. Our focus is bringing restoration to the lives of men and families in our community. We work at changing lives and restoring families.

Shalom specialises in two key areas; transforming lives and showing families how to bring a person to the point of wanting to change. At the same time, we put things in place to protect the family in order to minimise the damage to the hearts and lives of those concerned.

> *"You can lead a horse to water, but you can't make it drink."*

No-one can change me except me, and no-one can change you except you.

Most people have heard of the saying, "You can lead a horse to water, but you can't make it drink."

No-one can change anyone except the person themselves. We are where we are because of the choices we make.

Every circumstance we face determines a choice that we make that will give us an outcome. We all face circumstances we do and don't create, but at the end of the day, we are the ones that determine how we respond to those circumstances that we face.

Change starts by making a choice, "I want to change."

However, the question we need to ask is, "How do we get a person to make that choice?"

Let me explain in the shortest way possible.

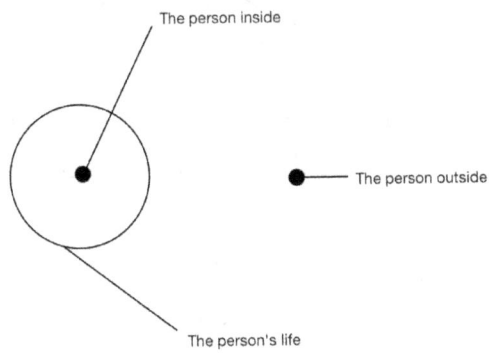

Draw a circle, and put a dot on the inside and a dot on the outside. If that circle represented a person's life, the dot on the inside was a person and the dot on the outside was a person, who is more qualified to see what's happening in the middle of the circle? Is it the person on the inside or the person on the outside?

Most people say that it's the person on the inside because they're living their life — they can see what's happening. But in reality, it's the person on the outside. Sometimes it takes a person on the outside to show a person on the inside what it is that they can't see.

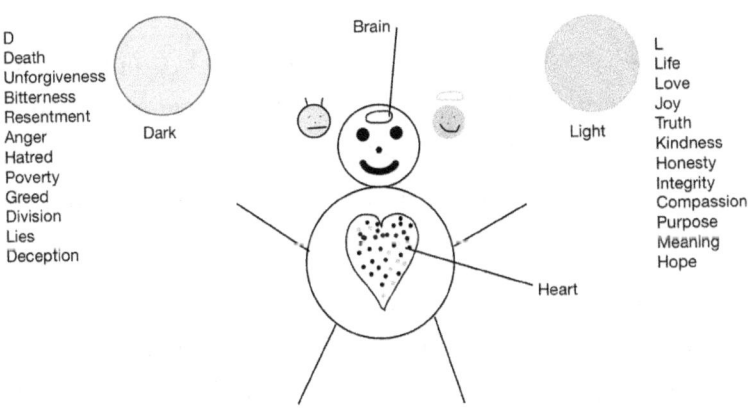

Now there are two types of forces at work in this world.

A light and a dark, a good and a bad, a God and a Devil, and each one produces fruit.

If the light were to be light, most people believe that the light would be good and if the dark were dark, most people believe it would be bad.

Light (L) = Life, love, truth, joy, kindness, honesty, integrity, compassion, purpose, meaning, builds togetherness, gives hope, it unites families together and brings life.

Dark (D) = death, unforgiveness, bitterness, resentment, anger, hatred, poverty, division, it conquers and it destroys. It separates families and turns them against each other and brings death.

Neither one of these two forces can violate our free will; however, both will follow us throughout the course of our life, giving us a choice to follow or listen to either one. Both are trying to enter us to influence us and when we give them permission, they produce fruit.

The dark, D, produces bad fruit, and the light, L, produces good fruit. Picture drinking a cup of poison filled with everything full of the D and the influence it would have on you, what would come out of your mouth and then picture the same with the L. The opposite would occur.

The second that we are born, we begin to be programmed. How we are programmed is, by the way, Dad is Dad in the home, the way he treats Mum, the way our parents model parenthood, the way they are with their money, as well as the way they respond and communicate to people they deal with on a daily basis. We are also being programmed by the schools that we go to and by the people we meet, by the circumstances that we face, both good and bad.

As we face certain circumstances, we make choices about how to respond as well as setting boundaries in our life to protect us from the same things happening again. Through it all, we continually make choices that we allow into our hearts that make us who we are today.

Of course, no-one in their right mind would allow the D to enter, but unintentionally we do. Once we do, what's in us operates through us as well as influences us as to who we are as a person.

Your heart is the hard drive

Your heart is the hard drive that holds all this information, both good and bad. There is a proverb that speaks about "Out of the heart flows the issues (consequences) of life" (Matthew 5:19).

We are supposed to guard our hearts (Proverbs 4:23) as it is the wellspring of life. It is from where we draw our wisdom, strength and knowledge. The heart can also be deceitful beyond all measure (Jeremiah 17:9) and sometimes cannot be trusted, because out of your heart, your mouth speaks (Matthew 15:18).

> *"I had opened up so many doors to my heart because of what I went through, most of what I believed was a lie; especially what I believed about myself and others."*

My programme (my heart) so to speak, when growing up, was all stuffed up. My heart was totally damaged and broken because of what I went through as a child and then as an adult. I had opened up so many doors to my heart because of what I went through, most of what I believed was a lie, especially what I believed about myself and others.

I believed that no-one loved me, that I was useless, that at times, everyone else was to blame for how I was, that I couldn't be like normal people, like I didn't belong or fit in. Yet I believed with all my heart that I was right in what I felt or believed about myself, even though other people were telling me I was wrong. If a person believes with all of their heart that they are right, when in actual fact, they are wrong — that person is deceived. It's really hard to convince a person they are wrong when they believe they are right. Sometimes you have to allow a person from the outside of the circle to show the person on the inside what it is that they can't see. You need to replace the lie with the truth, and as you do, the fruit of their life will change.

The picture on page 21 shows a little fat man; he has a brain, eyes, nose and mouth and in his tummy is the hard drive to his life, his heart. On the left, there is a D, and on the right, there is an L; on the left, there is a demon, and on the right, there is an angel. That little fat man is living life with both of those forces following him, wanting the person to produce fruit. The light wants him to produce good fruit and the dark, bad fruit.

When you face both good and bad circumstances, they both whisper. One says, "Forgive," and the other says, "Ignore him, don't forgive."

On another occasion, the little fat man walks into a service station and pays for his fuel and the operator gives him $20 too much change.

One voice says, "Stuff him, you've scored!"

The other says, "Give it back; it's not yours."

Every decision we make in life has a consequence, and we will either pay now or later, but we will pay.

A personal insight

As a child from the age of seven to nine, events turned from bad to worse in my life. My dad took off when I was seven years old, and I hadn't seen him for a couple of years. For the next two years, it felt like my whole family was destroyed, broken up and dissolved. I had been abused sexually by a friend's uncle, rejected and abandoned. I felt scared and alone. Dad had abandoned me and Mum had given up on me.

I hadn't seen my Dad in over two years, and the police had caught me sleeping in a Good Samaritan collection bin at the Midland Gate shopping centre. They took me back to Parkerville Children's Home. On arrival back at the office of the home, I was surprised to find my Dad was waiting there. I hadn't seen him in well over two years since he abandoned me.

> *"I remember agreeing with the lie by saying, 'Yeah, that's right,' and I felt something go from my head to my heart and an overwhelming anger come on me towards my Dad."*

The counsellor sat to my left and my Dad to my right.

The counsellor said to me, "Peter, you obviously don't want to be here anymore, we are going to give you a choice. Go and stay with your Dad or go to Longmore."

I heard one voice say in my ear, "Go to your Dad's," and the other said straight away, "Stuff him, he doesn't love you anymore."

My brain processed what was said, checked with the damage in my heart and it felt true, even though now I know it to be a lie.

I remember agreeing with the lie by saying, "Yeah, that's right," and I felt something go from my head to my heart and an overwhelming anger come upon me towards my Dad.

From that day forward, I hated him with a passion.

I said to the lady, "I'll go to Longmore."

Now these black dots and scars that are on the heart should not be there. What the D does is sow them deep into the hard drive of your heart. For me, that one about my Dad had a strong hold on my life. That gave the D permission to put more and more strongholds (beliefs) on my heart because he already had a root to build upon. The more strongholds he has in a person, the easier it is to enter and soon it is much easier to listen to the D than it is to the L.

TOUGH LOVE

CHAPTER

~3~

Understanding Ice

Methamphetamine, what an evil drug! It opens the floodgates to the heart, corrupting and damaging it at a rate never seen before by any other drug. The person on the drug becomes a Trojan Horse of evil. Their heart is so damaged and broken because of the choices they have made and the life they have lived, and then families take that person into their home, noooo! What a mistake that is.

Normal everyday families try to help a person who is on meth and depending where that person is at depends on how much families have to deal with. What I've done below is put together tools in order to show what stage of addiction they are at, as well as some tips about what should be done.

What to look for

I get hundreds of calls from families reaching out on behalf of a loved one they know is using drugs, but they don't know what to do or how to help. Often the calls are from families who have no idea about drugs or their warning signs. They ring me up saying their son or daughter has been using marijuana or synthetic cannabis and they need help. They then go on to explain what their child is going through, which 90 percent of the time are symptoms of a person who is using methamphetamine.

Yet because they have no experience with the drug, they don't know what to look for and therefore have no idea. I call those families "geeks", or normal people. My whole life I wanted to be a geek, a normal person, living a normal life. Doing normal things like attending one school, living at home with Mum and Dad, going on family holidays, sitting at the table as a family having dinner, playing sport, not getting drunk or smoking – a normal person. Today I'm a geek.

Here are some of the things you can look out for when trying to see if a person is on meth.

Dryness around the mouth	Always borrowing money or selling off assets
Dilated pupils	Picking at their skin for no reason
Jaw clenching and grinding	They eat lots of chocolate and candy
Talk a lot and seem to tell some very doubtful stories	Always coming up with ways to make big bucks
Stay awake all hours of the night for a few days running, then sleep all day	Always angry, the slightest comment can trip them off
They disappear at odd hours and come home late	The circle of friends they have has changed for the worse
Paranoid, they believe that people are following them	They start missing days off work and start becoming consistently late
Short tempered	Many cases they have sores all over themselves that they can't stop scratching or picking at
Agitated, rude and quick to fly off the handle about nothing	They start messing around with gadgets, phone chargers for hours
Always blames others for the way they are like they are	When they do disappear for a few days, they only come back to sleep
Their body odour starts to change and has a chemical smell to it	
They seem to avoid you so that you can't see the obvious	
Always telling lies, you sense it, but just can't seem to prove it	

Where are they at in regards to addiction

You can work out what stage a person is at in regards to addiction by identifying what stage of addiction they are at. When you have identified where they are at you can then put together a response or an action plan depending on the stage that the individual is at. There are so many scenarios that I could use to give examples to help understand what to do and how to handle it but many things must be taken into consideration.

For example, they are a:

- Married man with children
- Single man in a de facto relationship
- 16-year-old person living at home with parents
- 36-year-old person living at home with parents
- Person not living at home
- Single mum with children
- Young, unmarried couple with the woman pregnant
- Parent concerned about a child with addiction

Or:

- Does the person have a history of drug use?
- Are they a couple and are they both using drugs?
- Is he using drugs and not her?

You can class a person's stage of addiction by using the following chart. It is made up of five stages; A, B, C, D and E. Now depending on what stage a person is at determines which course of action you would take to help that person.

Stages of Addiction

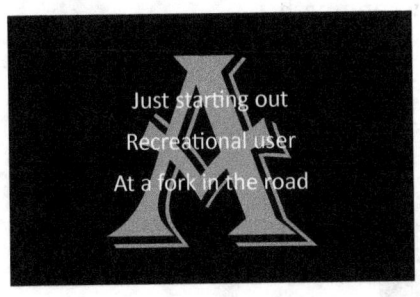

Just starting out
Recreational user
At a fork in the road

is a person who is first starting on the pathway to drugs. A young person is hitting the age of fourteen, going okay at school, but is facing the challenges of puberty, etc. He or she goes out to a party and sees a heap of other kids having a good time, one of them is smoking cones, and the young person gets offered one. Before they try the drug, in their head one voice says, "Go on, have one, everyone else is doing it," with the other voice saying, "Don't be stupid, you know it's wrong."

Often, with a bit of peer pressure, they make the wrong choice and try it. Depending on the individual and the effects it has on them, this will determine if they continue its use. There are many people who have a very bad experience the first time they use drugs and vow never to use it again. There are also many who love the euphoria of the effects the drugs give them and find a new sense of purpose and strength to fit in, something that they never had before.

Our experience at Shalom House has been that many of my fellas who were at that stage when they were young were facing problems at home or something had happened to them that they couldn't or wouldn't talk to anyone about. We have had many fellas who have experienced bullying as a child; they have never really fitted in with the cool kids. Then one day they go to a party, and the cool kids were using drugs, and with a bit of pressure, they tried some and found a level of acceptance from their peers that they had never had before, encouraging them down the wrong path.

is someone who has accepted using drugs recreationally and sees no harm in it, as "everyone else is doing it." They say, "I'm not hurting anyone, it's no different than having a beer."

Every weekend, they make it the standard norm to go out with their mates, have a few cones and just consider it the weekend's usual activity. B's are pretty hard to turn around or talk to as they see no harm in what they are doing. They have made their choice; it's okay, they say. The euphoria that the drug gives you far outweighs the guilt of making wrong choices. Deception starts at A and settles into the heart here. Again, if a person believes a lie as truth, that lie becomes their truth.

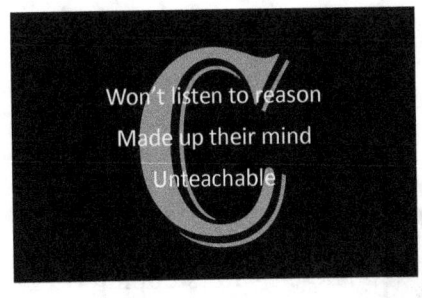 is someone who just doesn't listen. They have chosen the path they are taking and are now doing drugs on a daily basis. They wind down at the end of the day by having a few cones, a couple of beers and have started trying other drugs. Marijuana cones are the standard normal during the week, and the heavier drugs are now the weekend delight. The same cycle continues with the heavier drugs that they did with the pot.

They say, "I only do it on weekends."

"I'm not hurting anyone."

"It's only Friday and Saturday."

"It's only every fortnight."

"I'm okay."

But over time, the use escalates to a point where they can't stop if they tried. Cones are now a thing of the past, meth (ice) or hammer (heroin) is now the drug of choice. Weekly usage now moves to daily, there's no stopping now.

Slowly the identity of the person starts to change, the friends they have, the way they talk. You can see the person changing and you start to have suspicions that things aren't quite the same, but you can't put your finger on it. You approach the individual to raise some of your concerns, but they come up with an explanation you accept as reasonable, but deep down you know it's not. They start to become unreliable, taking longer to do certain tasks, asking for short-term loans, talking a lot more than they used to and showing symptoms of paranoia. Cs & Ds are the most destructive, not just on the person, but also the families and all involved, both directly and indirectly.

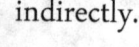

There's no stopping a D as the use of drugs is now daily, with the heavier drugs being the drug of choice. People around them can see them changing, and yet the user is blinded to the changes taking place inside them. If they were not blinded, they would not refuse to look or listen to people who point out the obvious. Everything about them is changing, the way they speak, the way they treat those around them, their morals and values aren't the same anymore, their priorities and the people they are hanging around, everything. Financially they are starting to fall apart, loans and bills are not getting paid on time, they start to ask family members for small loans, making excuses why they need the money and are continually having to cover their tracks as to why.

Their use of drugs starts to get so bad they are missing work because they did not wake up in time, and when they are at work, the quality of their work is no longer the same. The employer sees a massive change in the person; their ability to cope and get work done in the workplace is no longer there. Their moods are so bad now it seems that everyone in the home has to tiptoe around on eggshells so as not to upset the drug-affected family member. People can clearly see the drug's effects on a D and they try to bring truth to the user, but the user will not have a bar of it. They consider it an attack and start to blame the person bringing the truth. The user blames them for the circumstances that they are in and somehow it gets turned back on the person trying to help. The user blames you or others for the way that they are, no matter what you say, they think they are not at fault. What is really saddening is that families honestly only know 10 percent of what is going on and are left to give advice knowing very little of what is really happening.

Everything has come to a head, the person has lost their job, been kicked out of home, or has been forcibly removed from the home by police and restraining orders have been put in place. The bills can no longer get paid as the source of funds has finally dried up. The family support has stopped because it's been financially exhausted. The user is at the bottom of the bottom of the bottom. They ring you up crying for help, saying they are ready to change, they finally admit that they need help and tell you everything you want to hear in order for them to get what they need to get.

What they say answers a whole heap of what you were thinking and also a whole heap of what you presumed. Again, the series of stuff that unfolds depends on the person's circumstances and background. What I see quite often with an E is the wife, for example, has had enough. Husband is an E, he has hit the wall and the wife has been brought to the point where she has no choice but to get hubby forcibly removed from the home. So, Mum and Dad, in their stupidity, try to step in and intervene by bringing their son back into their home.

The cycle then continues again except that because of the break and a new roof over his head, he has now dropped back to a C or a D. Because of the parent's lack of insight as to what he has been up to, he brings his bad stuff to their home and then his bad stuff over time spreads onto them. They start to experience what the wife went through and over time, he picks up speed and becomes an E again.

Finally, Mum and Dad have to have him removed from the property. The problem is that after he has gone or been removed from the property, the marriage between the two parents is never the same again. This is because Mum and Dad end up with unforgiveness and bitterness in their hearts towards each other, as well as towards their son. Mum said to do it this way and Dad said to do it that way; it brings massive amounts of division into the family unit, some of whom never recover.

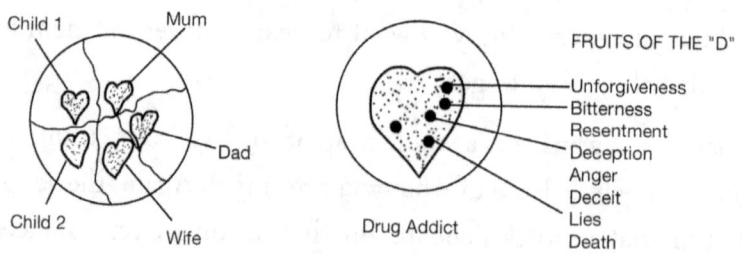

How to bring correction

How you would bring correction to an A, B or C for the first time?

Obviously when you find out a person is doing something wrong, you tell them off and give them a warning. If they do it the second time, you not only tell them off, but you also give them a consequence. The third time, you must hand them over to the consequences of their choices.

Remember, you are dealing with drugs; meth and ice must be treated differently. To help the person, you must understand the drug, in order to treat the drug.

In order for any home to work, it must have non-negotiable rules for it to function as a normal home should. Everyone within the home must respect those rules, otherwise it will fall apart.

One of those rules must be NO DRUGS on or off the property.

If a family member can't abide by that rule, then it is not the place for them, plain and simple. When I say plain and simple, you would think it would be that easy, but sadly, many families do not have what it takes to do that. Most families can't stand the thought of their loved one living on the street, so they take them in, therefore, they learn the hard way.

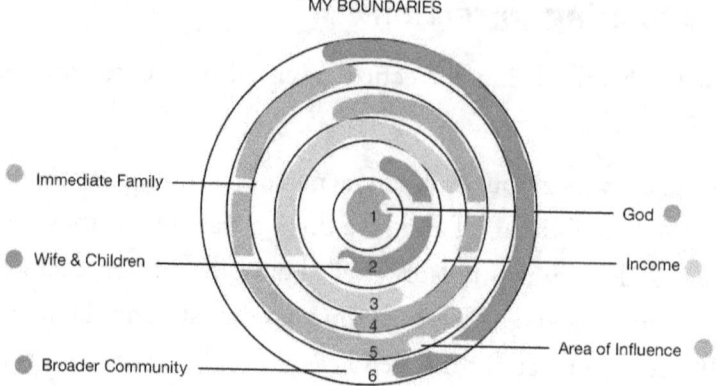

The diagram above is like a dartboard and it shows the boundaries that I set for myself and my family. The first circle is myself and God, the second circle is my wife and children, the third circle is the income that supports the two inner circles, the fourth circle is my extended family, the fifth is my area of influence and the sixth is beyond into the broader community.

If my middle circle is not functioning properly, I drop everything else off outside of it and make it my focus until it is fixed. It's the same with the second, third and fourth, etc. For you, your circles might be different.

When a person is over the age of sixteen, they are classed as an adult and are responsible for their own choices. If they wish to stay in the home, they must agree not to use drugs, which is not an unreasonable request. The first time you catch them using, warn them.

Let them know you do not want drugs or a drug user in the home and that it's not okay to use drugs on or off the property.

Warn them of the consequences that will unfold if they don't listen.

If you catch them using a second time, you need to look at the circumstances surrounding what took place and issue consequences accordingly. You will also need to establish boundaries to deal with it and to prevent it happening again, such as random urine tests, counselling, etc.

Explain to them that if there is a third time, then you will have no other choice other than to ask them to leave the family home.

This is a MUST when dealing with drugs or a drug addict, especially if a person is on meth or other heavy drugs like heroin. If you don't get them to leave, that person's choice to use drugs brings a Trojan Horse of evil into your home that spreads over time to every family member. If you don't act sooner rather than later, you will end up learning the hard way.

If you know me, I would be the first to knock on your door to say, "I told you so."

Remember the third time, KICK THEM OUT, but do so in love.

You say, "Fred, I warned you three times, now I have no other choice but to ask you to leave."

If you don't do this, I know without doubt that you will live to regret it. Normally even at the first stage when you catch them using, it's been going on for a very, very long time, but you've discovered it too late. Believe me when I say you will move through the three warnings very quickly as you know only five percent of what they have been up to. By the time you do discover they're on drugs, the person is already at the D level.

Meth is an evil drug, it changes the person.

Remember you're not dealing with a person anymore, you're dealing with the drug and in order to help the person, you must treat the drug.

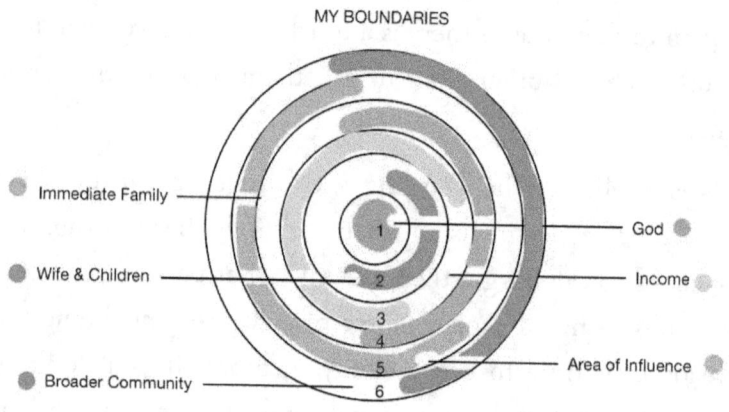

Again, if you want to know how to check if you are making the right choice, put your finger to the far right, outside all the circles. Now picture that your finger is the person affected by drugs. Move your finger slowly towards the centre circle, but stop where you think things might go pear-shaped, if that person was in that circle.

By doing that, it should show you where it is that you need to set the boundaries. You are mad taking that person closer to the centre, as you will only take yourself and others out in the process.

> ***"If you continue to spare them from the consequences of those choices, they will never learn."***

That's a good indication that you are making a right choice – don't trust them or let them into your centre circles. If you really want to help them now, you MUST help them from a distance. Remember, they are where they are because of their choices. If you continue to spare them from the consequences of those choices, they will never learn.

If you allow them into your circle, I know that it's only a matter of time before their stuff becomes your stuff. You come to the point where you have no other choice except to kick them out of the home and more often than not, it's by the police. When it gets to that stage, you're normally at a place where the last thing you want to do is to help them. You don't want to get there because then you're no good for anybody, especially them.

A Short Story

Imagine a boat load of eighty people going from Perth to China. The boat is full and every person on it has just enough supplies (water and food) to get them there, with none to spare. You're halfway across the ocean and there are hundreds of people stuck in the water, waving at you to wanting to get into the boat.

In one man's hand is a year's supply of food that has been contaminated.

You yell at him to let go of the food, but he says, "No, please let me in, I'm drowning."

If the food comes on board, it will contaminate everyone else, but he still refuses to let go. Do you let him in? Of course not.

It's no different with drugs; if the person refuses to stop, throw them out.

Don't feel guilty

From a distance, you can protect yourself and other family members and encourage them to make right choices. Don't feel guilty about the decisions you are making. If you follow the warning process and you have laid all your cards on the table, they should understand the rules. You must be strong, be prepared for a long battle. This way is 90 percent faster if you can get everyone on the same page and it protects everyone from a lot of unnecessary hurt and speeds up the process.

Bring the truth in love

Whatever you do, don't communicate out of emotion, don't yell or scream at them, keep calm and try to bring the truth in love. If you yell and scream at them, they will have the "D" voice whispering to their mind, "They don't love you anymore," or "They hate you," or "They're judging you."

If he or she believes that lie, it goes from the head into the heart, and it produces fruit that further ostracises them from you and the rest of the family.

It pushes them away from you when all you want is for them to come to you. The drug has a way of turning the people you love the most into the people you hate the most, it causes you to blame others for how you are and why you are the way you are.

No-one likes to kick their child out on the street or watch them suffer, but unless you do, they will die and other people will get hurt in the process.

When dealing with a meth addict, I try to encourage families to look at it as if the person has cancer, except we have a cure. What I am trying to give you is the cure for this type of cancer. No-one likes to undergo radiation therapy or chemo but unless you do, there is a strong chance you will die. Have you ever sat with a person who has cancer? All you can do is try to make them comfortable and encourage them to make right choices, to think good thoughts, drive them to appointments and care for them as best as possible.

> **"No-one likes to kick their child out on the street or watch them suffer, but unless you do, they will die, and other people will get hurt in the process."**

I know sooner or later you will have no choice as it will come to that point. What's sad is a number of others got hurt because you failed to act sooner. You really need to be encouraged right now to look at it differently.

You're NOT being mean by putting them out on the streets. You're giving them the cure for cancer. You're speeding up the process and helping them come to the point of wanting to change.

People say, "I can't kick them out — what happens if they die?"

Well, they are dying anyway, very slowly and you are helping them to do it. Not only are they dying, but they are taking others out in the process. They are sticking battery acid in their veins, for crying out loud. They are inhaling toxic fumes that are tripping out their brains and doing mental damage that many people may never fully recover from. Many addicts affected by meth threaten family members with committing suicide.

Yes, that is a very real possibility, and in some cases, it does happen. I have sat with mothers who have lost their children to suicide. I have sat with wives who have lost their husbands. Despite these tragic events, I will still stand by my advice and will not change my stance as I know that this process works. Worst case, you may lose a loved one to drugs. Best case scenario, you might save them from a lifetime of addiction, saving yourself and others from a lifetime of being at their memorial service. You will also save yourself from losing your own life and other people's lives in the process.

Also, please try to remember that meth and other drugs are very enjoyable. The feelings and euphoria that they give you are amazing, enjoyable and highly addictive. Depending on the drug, of course, depends on the effects that it gives you and in most cases, it's an instant relief from any problem that you are facing.

For drug users, the quickest way to fix a problem is to stick a pick in your arm, smoke a pipe or pop a pill – the second you do, the problem goes away. When you do that regularly over one year, five years, ten years or more, you are developing patterns of thinking and behaviour that you will need to relearn all over again. It's not just as easy to say stop using drugs because the individual needs to relearn communication skills, dealing with conflict, expressing how they feel, the decision-making processes and much, much more all over again.

Why don't you give them a urine test, then?

If you're unsure if a person is on drugs, or think they are, but want to know which one, then the best way to know for sure is to urine test them. You can get a urine test kit from your local chemist for about thirty dollars. It's best to get the best test kit they sell and the one that tests for all drugs, because if you're going to do it, you may as well do it properly.

When urine testing them, there are a few things you need to do to make sure they don't deceive you and also how to minimise confrontation. Drug addicts are very smart in knowing how to get away with faking or not taking drug tests. The last thing you want to do is give them any notice about what you're about to do or planning on doing. People go to extremes to avoid giving a dirty sample.

What I used to do was get someone who I knew was clean to pee into a balloon for me. After they had peed in it, I'd tie a knot in the balloon and put a safety pin hole in it where the dimple was, then keep it stored under my groin so that I could keep it at body temperature. When I walked in to give the test, I would face the toilet, grab the balloon and then squeeze it into the cup. As it came out, it sounded like pee, it was at room temperature and it didn't look suspicious because of the way that I did it.

Avoiding Tests

There are many ways to avoid a test. When you spring a test on them and they swear black and blue that they can't pee no matter how hard they try, don't believe them and refuse to take no for an answer. I tell them that I will not be leaving their company in any way, shape or form until they pee and if they can't pee, I tell them that I will treat the pee as a dirty test.

This will automatically find them guilty, therefore handing them over to the consequences. Sadly, many of them accept that and use it against you later on, they continue to declare they were innocent and that you were wrong, even though in your heart you felt you were right. Guilty until proven innocent, I say.

Oh, and make sure you watch them, don't let them out of your sight until you get the sample. If they can't pee, then be near water and turn the tap on, the sound of running water helps a person to pee. I know, it affects me like that every time I fill my car with petrol (too much information, right?).

How to confront them

Try to get them after they have had a sleep because if you try to test them when they are pinging off their head, you will find it will just end in all-out confrontation and that's what you want to avoid if you can.

How you would ask would be something like this:

"Jay, I don't mean to be disrespectful and I don't want to be rude. I don't want to have a go at you or do anything that hurts you in any way. I want you to know that I really care about you and about where your life is heading. I don't want to control you, but want to help you. I've been thinking for some time now that you're going through a bit of stuff as you're not the same anymore and I want to be there for you; not in the way you want me to, but in a way that I know that I need to.

I have some concerns, and I know that there may be a possibility that I am wrong, and if I am, then I want to say I'm sorry. But if I'm not, I want to work out the best way to help you. I have a strong suspicion that you are using drugs of some kind and I want to know what one so I would like to ask if you would be prepared to provide a urine sample for me?

I'm sorry to have to ask, but I'm not prepared to take no for an answer as I know something is not right and in order for me to know what to do and how to help you and myself, I need to know what drugs I'm up against."

Keep your eye on them

It's really important when you urine test a person that you keep your eye on them, watch them when they pee. Don't let them have any notice and don't let them pee into the jar unsupervised. If they are on drugs, they can't be trusted; you're not dealing with your loved one anymore, you're dealing with the drug. Many people, when trying to help an individual, do so by treating the person when they should be treating the drug, BIG mistake.

Now what...?

Once you have got your sample, now test it. The result of the reading will determine the course of action that you must take. There is a great deal to take into consideration when planning a suitable course of action, but the next step would be to try to work out where they are at in regards to their addiction. Depending on that would determine the course of action, but at least now you know what you're dealing with.

The family dynamics, what drugs they're using and where a person is at, as well as at what stage they are, will determine how the family should handle the problem and what they should do. Later on in this book, I have provided some helpful examples using some of the email and texts that I have received from individuals who have contacted me about people caught up in addictions.

Working together

If I were to hold up five fingers and each one of those fingers was to represent an option, the first being the decision to change your life, the second your wife or partner, the third your parents, the fourth your grandparents or another family member and the fifth is a best mate or friend of the family.

What I find is that the person will never ever make the decision to change their life as long as you spare them the consequences of their choices. When dealing with a person on meth, you must understand the drug. You're not dealing with the person; you're dealing with the drug.

The first finger is the decision to change your life, that's the ideal outcome for every family; wouldn't it be easy if everyone automatically made that choice? But in reality, for level Cs & Ds, it's very unlikely and for the E, a strong possibility, depending on how the family handle it. What I find is the majority of families think they are doing the right thing, but in actual fact, they are doing the wrong thing. You will find that I refer to the stages of addiction often and will be dealing mostly with the C, D & E stages.

I received an email on behalf of a lady who was reaching out for her brother-in-law. How to tell where he is at is very easy, he's an E. I want the Es to come to me at Shalom House, as long as there are no other fingers up (options). I can help the Es and with the families' help, I can show them how to get them there. This diagram shows how it works.

Somehow, I need to get the mind thinking, "I can't do this anymore, I want to change."

When the mind creates that thought, which I call a seed, "I can't do this anymore," and then makes its mind up, "I want to change," that seed goes from the head to the heart.

When they come and see me, I can tell if that seed is there in the heart. I can water that seed, I can make it grow. I know how to make it grow, that's good seed. Once the seed is there, then begins the process of cleaning up the heart.

"So a man thinks in his heart, so is he." (Proverbs 23:7)

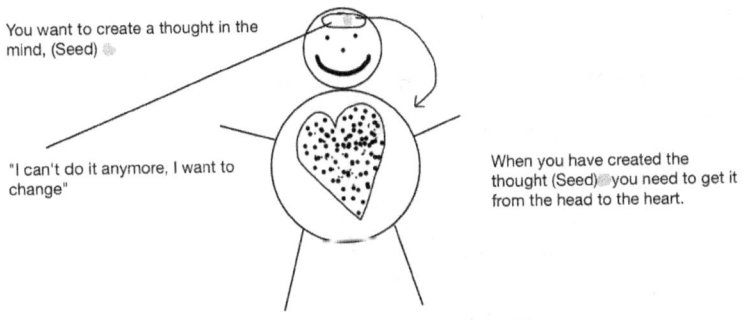

You want to create a thought in the mind, (Seed)

"I can't do it anymore, I want to change"

When you have created the thought (Seed) you need to get it from the head to the heart.

Until that thought (Seed) is in the heart the person will NEVER change.

This is an email I received not long ago.

I'm just enquiring about your programme for my brother-in-law, Jay. He is 31 years old and has been struggling with a drug addiction. Yesterday it reached a crisis point when he was violent towards his partner in front of their two children. She has now left him and he will no doubt continue to seek more drugs as he goes on this downward spiral. We have evidence that he has been using ice as well as marijuana. He also smokes cigarettes and drinks alcohol. Jay has a beautiful heart but is not himself. He has probably been battling addictions from around the age of 13.

His parents don't know what to do. He has begged for money from them, as well as from his brothers. He comes from a big, supportive, loving family who all want to help him, but don't know quite what to do.

Let's break it down

Jay is an E and what has just taken place would have been building up for some time.

His partner would have failed to act because of a few reasons such as, "I never dreamed I'd be a single mum."

"I don't want to be single."

"How am I going to pay the rent?"

"What about the mortgage?"

"How am I going to survive with two kids?"

"What will people think of me?"

"How is this going to affect the children?"

What should have happened is that she should have made a stand a long time ago, well before this, when he was a B. People don't want to speak up due to all the shame that comes with it. Many people nowadays are treating ice the same as pot or speed, but it's not; it's in a league of its own. It's the most destructive drug ever to hit humanity, it's evil and it destroys families at a rapid rate. When dealing with a person on meth, you're not dealing with the person any longer, you're dealing with the drug.

Now in this case, his partner left him, but most of the time when children are concerned, he gets forcibly removed by the police and a restraining order gets put in place. Mum and Dad in their stupidity try to step in and help, they allow Jay into their home as he has no place else to go. Oh, what a mistake that is, they will learn the hard way. Imagine bringing a treasure chest of evil into your home; bitterness, unforgiveness, jealousy, hatred, addiction, lies, deceit, just to name a few. Have a look at the illustration on page 53 as this represents Mum and Dad with Jay now back at home with the rest of the family.

"We need to get him to the bottom of the bottom so that his mind will start to generate a seed, a seed that says, 'I can't do this anymore.'"

All those dots represent all the stuff that should not be there and you have now brought that into your home. Oh, my God, a Trojan horse full of evil. You are not qualified to help your son, not in the way that you want to anyway, get him out of the home ASAP. The last thing you should do is to allow him in your home, what we need to do is leave him out on the streets.

We need to get him to the bottom of the bottom so that his mind will start to generate a seed, a seed that says, "I can't do this anymore."

When the seed is made, we need to put it in the heart and bring him to the point where, of his own accord, he comes to a point where he says, "I want to change."

What tends to happen when Mum and Dad do bring him into the home, he divides the house, Mum says, "Do it this way," and Dad says, "Do it this way."

The parents start to argue a great deal and bitterness, resentment, unforgiveness and division enter their hearts. Fear spreads into the hearts of the rest of the family living in the home and now his stuff has become everyone else's stuff and the family is never the same again. They all find themselves walking around on eggshells until they get brought to the point where they have no choice, but to kick him out.

What he leaves behind is the family struggling to recover from the effects of having him in the home and many never do.

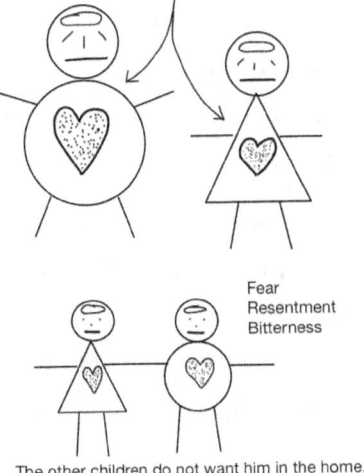

Division.
Mum says do it this way and Dad says this way.

Fear
Resentment
Bitterness

The other children do not want him in the home.

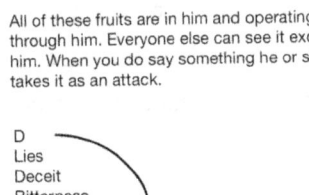

All of these fruits are in him and operating through him. Everyone else can see it except him. When you do say something he or she takes it as an attack.

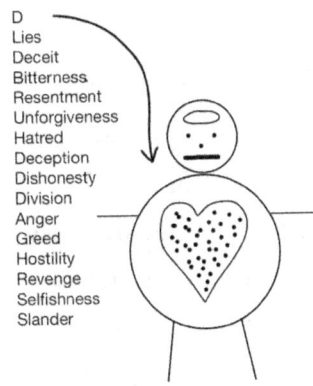

D
Lies
Deceit
Bitterness
Resentment
Unforgiveness
Hatred
Deception
Dishonesty
Division
Anger
Greed
Hostility
Revenge
Selfishness
Slander

I've sat with many families who have separated because of what Jay brought into the home. Mum just couldn't find it within her to kick her son out, so the whole family went down in the process. So sad, so very, very sad. You will see a real-life example of this in the coming pages.

Most families would know who Jay would run to (brothers, grandma), who the other fingers are, so to speak. What you need to do is get everyone together; get them on the same page. Nominate a team leader, one who is strong enough to call the shots, someone able to stand firm when hard choices have to be made. When you kick Jay out, no-one put a roof over his head whatever you do. What he is doing is wrong, he has gone past the point of listening, otherwise he would have listened a long time ago; you need to bring him to the end of himself.

You will find that he will more than likely go into self-destruct mode, blaming you and everyone else for the way he is. Don't listen to that, protect your heart, it's lies. There is no truth in it; he is where he is because of his choices. He has no-one else to blame except himself, don't let him guilt-trip you into feeling bad. Sure, over the course of your life, you may have made some mistakes and done things wrong.

But even though you did, he is the one who has made the choice to feel or to believe or act the way he does. For many years, I held onto unforgiveness towards my parents for the way that I was and for what I went through as a child, but I realised one day that I was to blame for where I was at. I was holding onto unforgiveness and bitterness and out of the anger and resentment I had in my heart, I made a series of choices that sent my life further in the wrong direction.

I'm not saying you should give up on him, but rather set yourself some boundaries to protect yourself and other people who live in the home, otherwise over time, you will be no good for anyone. Learn how to bring the truth in love, never communicate out of emotion as it will only come back at you and increase the chances of the Dark getting deeper into his heart. So, what you do is set yourself some boundaries, don't let him or her into your circle and be prepared to help from a distance.

What you should do

- Give good advice – Remember you can't change the person, but you can be there, united with them in the choices that they make. Don't push your advice on them but rather present it. If they ask for it.

- Set yourself up for the long term – What you need to remember is that this may be an ongoing problem that will take some time to rectify or come through. Be prepared mentally and emotionally for a hard road ahead.

- Encourage them to make right choices – again, you can lead a horse to water, but you can't make it drink. Encouraging them in making right choices without doing anything physically for them is the way to go, as it keeps the ball in their court.

- Set yourself some boundaries – You really need to sit down with your partner and put some boundaries in place. Identify what you are prepared to do and also what you should not do. When you have identified your boundaries get some wise counsel about what you are about to put in place. Some of the boundaries might be: to not pay any bills, not allowing him or her to live in the home, as well as how to respond to certain situations as they unfold.

- Guard your heart – whatever you do, guard your heart. Don't allow bitterness, resentment, unforgiveness, anger or anything that lines up with the D into your heart. Push it off, don't let it in, because if you do, it will change you as a person and I know you don't want that type of change.

- Find someone to download to – It's important that you have a close friend, pastor or counsellor that you can download to, but at the same time, they must be on the same page, otherwise it will just create confusion in your mind and you don't want that. Sometimes too much counsel can create more problems than it's worth. By having a safe place to download to, it helps you also to process your thoughts and to gain some clarity about what you are going through and about the decisions you are making.

- Minimise what you actually do on their behalf – you really need to minimise what you do on behalf of the person, as you want to make sure the ball is in their court as much as possible. If you do everything for them, it's more about you and what you want, rather than about the person and them wanting the change. I believe the extent of what you do is governed by how many times they have been where they are. In other words, is this the first, second or third warning/time they have been given before? (Third time = do nothing. First time = ring around and help them.)

- Each step of the way, put the ball in their court – You can't be led by what you feel or desire as it puts the ball in your court and not in theirs. They MUST be the one wanting to change. Otherwise it just doesn't work.

- Prepare to be disappointed – You really need to lower your expectations of the person and expect for them to let you down. Expect that they will not show up for appointments, that they will lie to you and let you down consistently.

- Watch the thoughts you let into your mind – There will be a war going on in your mind. One voice says, "Do it this way," and the other, "that way", and sometimes it just does your head in and it really annoys you. Well, welcome to my world. You can often tell the origin of the thought by the fruit it will produce in your life. A good thought would produce good fruit and a bad thought, bad fruit. Unforgiveness for the long and short-term produces bad fruit like division. In contrast, forgiveness brings restoration and reconciliation. I think you get what I mean.

What you don't do

What you don't do would be determined by where the addict is at and if you have been here before, e.g. the first warning, second warning or third warning. I am basing the following on the second and third:

- Never pay any bills or lend money – believe it or not, it actually helps the person to make a choice to change when you don't pay their bills, as it works as a leverage tool in your favour. The more pressure they have on them, the more they can see that they need to change. You are mad if you pay their bills as it's like pouring money down the drain.

- In most cases, it just gives you a short-term fix, but you will find that by paying their bills, you have equipped them to go another round of doing what they shouldn't be doing. Even in cases where they say they have bikies and other clubs threatening them, do not pay. I must acknowledge that depending on the circumstances with clubs, sometimes it's better to pay them to get rid of them, but ONLY if you can have some guarantee that your money will not be wasted and the person will not go back to drugs.

- Never give them any money – never give them money of any kind as you will be just feeding the drug habit. I know of many families who, every week, go and do shopping for the person on drugs because they don't want to see them go hungry. Knowing this, the addict always uses their own money on drugs, because they know that the family will support them.

- Do NOT buy them food. Sure, take them out for a meal, but do not buy bags of food or top up phone credit, etc. for them, as all you are doing is prolonging the inevitable. You want to do all you can to bring them to the point that they can see they need to change.

- Don't feel bad – try not to feel guilty about doing the right thing. Yes, it is hard. Yes, it hurts having to make some of the decisions you will need to make, but what you are doing is the right thing. Plus, it HELPS them in the way that they need it and not in the way that they want it. They will yell and scream at you and play all types of mind games with you, but stand firm. Do not feel bad about doing the right thing.

- Don't ring around everywhere on their behalf – most organisations don't like it when family members ring on the person's behalf as it shows a lack of commitment by the person needing the help. It's always good when the person needing the help is the one on the end of the line.

- Don't drive them around paying drug debts – you really need to minimise the amount you are involved. Set your boundaries and always keep the ball in their court.

Now remember I did say that you don't give up on them, but rather, set some boundaries. If they ever ring you up hungry, offer to give them a food voucher for twenty dollars from Woolworths, one that is not redeemable for smokes or alcohol. If they say they need credit to ring around for help, then maybe once, possible twice, you would give them a ten-dollar recharge, but after that, you will start to see that you may be wasting your money.

Remember, don't pay their bills because all you are doing is slowing down what we want to happen. We want them to come to the end of themselves and having debt coming from all directions actually helps you to help them to come to the point to want to change their life.

How to work out where they are at

I receive many emails and texts from people wanting help and also wanting help for another person. Some of those emails and texts are shown below. I have spoken to all these people and will tell you what I see in each text. You may even see what you are going through here also.

Gavin

Pete, can you please ring me ASAP regarding my 24-year-old son Gavin? Needs me to give him $600 so some bikies don't throw him off a balcony or shoot him – to pay for drugs. I don't want to enable him. He said he will talk to you about turning *his life around, says he wants to change. I need wisdom. Any advice for me, please?*

Gavin is a D/E, everything around him is falling apart, bikies are chasing him for some cash and he is in fear for his life, a great place to be. What the Mum or Dad does from here is really important, they can either pay his bill bringing him back down to a C or D (a bad thing), or they can watch, stay strong and pray, set boundaries and be ready to give the right advice as it all unfolds.

But what she does from here may determine if he takes the next step or doesn't. The user will always try to bribe you by saying if you give me the cash or pay my bill, I'll do as you ask and seek help, whatever you do, don't listen to them, they're full of baloney. If they get the $600 bucks, he would go straight back to the drugs like a dog to its vomit and a pig to the mud.

Many times parents pay the bill, thinking they are doing the right thing, but are in fact doing the wrong thing. Many users will learn from the experience and do their best not to put themselves back in this position again, but they will go straight back to the drugs.

What she had to do is to say, "Sorry Gavin, I'm not going to help you in the way that you want me to, but in the way that I need to. I'm not giving you any money or paying any of your bills. Again, I'm not going to help you the way you want me to, but in the way that I need to."

Gavin is now in my rehab and has been for some time and is doing exceptionally well.

When dealing with a person off their face on drugs, one of the standard responses I tell families to say goes like this:

(Name)..... you know that I love you and always will, but I'm not qualified to help you. I am not going to be there for you in the way that you want me to, but rather in the way that I need to. You are a grown man now and are responsible for your choices. You need help, and unless you seek the help and follow it through to the end, you can't come back here. I am always happy to buy you a meal, but I will never give you money or pay any of your bills or do anything for you until you start to take the first steps. Here is a list of rehabs that I know can help you, pick one and get your life sorted out.

On page 62 is a list of rehabilitation centres located in Perth, Western Australia. I pass out this list out to many families who ring me asking for help. It's important that you do a bit of research on rehabilitation centres and have a list ready to hand out when the opportunity presents itself. Of course, depending on the state and country that you live in, the places we recommended would be different.

REHABILITATION CENTRES

Peter Lyndon-James Shalom House Ph: 0404 654 004	Wanada www.wanada.org.au Ph: (08) 6557 9400	AccordWest Ph: (08) 9534 7788
St Bartholomew's House Ph: (08) 9323 5101	B-Attitudes Ph: 0422 181 873	Dayak Davis Tenacious House Ph: 0435 817 147
Cyrinian House Ph: (08) 9302 2222	Holyoake Ph: (08) 9416 4444	Next Step Drug Rehabilitation Ph: (08) 9219 1919
Palmerston Association Inc. Ph: (08) 9328 7355	Ruah Community Services Ph: (08) 9485 3939	Salvation Army Bridge Program Ph: (08) 9227 8086
St Patrick's Community Support Ph: (08) 9430 4159	Pindari Ministries Ph: 0427 386 381	Paul Perion Teen Challenge Ph: 0421 428 226
WA Substance Users Association Ph: (08) 9321 2877		

Be Very Careful

Please be very careful when choosing a rehabilitation centre. Check out the programme and make sure that it sits with you and that you are comfortable with the programme they offer before you recommend it.

STAY AWAY from any rehabilitation centre that relies on prescription meds to change the person. Most addicts swap an illegal addiction for a legal one. Therefore you're not really helping them, but rather swapping one addiction for another. I don't agree with the use of benzodiazepines and other drugs to get a drug addict off drugs because they have an addictive nature and rely more on the drug/chemical to do what they should be doing. Cold turkey detox is the best way in my opinion.

Again, when detoxing a person, your method would depend on what it is you are detoxing them from, take alcohol, for example. When detoxing an alcoholic, it's important that you give them vitamins as well as Valium at least four to five times during the day, otherwise, they run a very high risk of seizures. There are some rehabs that you MUST stay away from.

TOUGH LOVE

CHAPTER ~4~

Coping With An Addict

My son needs help

Here is another letter from a mum who says that her son has reached his lowest point and is ready for change.

Hi Pete, I don't know which way to turn. My son needs help; he has reached his lowest point. Someone is coming over this morning to pick him up but we have nowhere to drop him. He has been on crystal meth but is off it now but there has been a series of relapses. The police removed him last night but he turned up on my doorstep at 2 o'clock this morning, crying that the drug has changed him. Will you take him? Someone can drop him off today. I am a Christian and have prayed for a way out. I know he is in good hands with you. I have followed your story for a very long time and have seen the wonderful things you have done for these men. I am pleading with you to please take him in. I understand how busy you must be but I have no other option but to ask if you will take on one more. He used to be a beautiful young man but has lost everything. (Narelle)

This is from a mum who is at the end of her rope with nowhere to turn, she knows what she needs to do but just can't seem to bring herself to do it. This may seem cold to some people but it works and it's the truth. Her son is a grown man now and is responsible for his choices; no-one can change him except him. He is going through what he is because of the choices he has made and as sad as it is, you need to throw him out on the street. If you want to stick battery acid in your veins, then there is a consequence and that consequence is that it will give you psychosis, destroy your heath and eventually leave you homeless and on the streets. He had plenty of warning up until now and should have known better. Some may say this is a bit cold but it's not, you're going to have to do it sooner or later because you will have no choice.

Many parents don't listen to me the first time until they get to a point where they have no choice. By then, the damage has spread to a lot of other family members because the parents failed to act sooner. When he rocked up back at the door, she should have called the cops on him again. He has just been issued a 24-hour move on notice where it said that he was not to come back to the property for 24 hours and here he is, six hours later.

You need to send a clear message to his brain, "I'm not tolerating this anymore."

If you don't, then you're not helping him or yourself. Things will only get worse until you bring him to the point where he makes the decision.

"I can't do this anymore, I want to change."

Come on, for crying out loud, help him come to that point, stop pussy-footing around — sometimes I feel like throwing the parents out on the street.

"You need to send a clear message to his brain, 'I'm not tolerating this anymore.'"

I get many, many calls like this from parents and people wanting to drop the person off to me and I tell them not to bother because when they come to me they are only coming because Mum or Dad has told them to. That won't work because the seed is not in the heart.

When I sit with them, I can see that they have two or three fingers up, meaning they have other options other than rehab, they will only last a few days with me and as soon as it starts to get hard, they run back to Mum or Dad knowing if they say the right things, Mum or Dad will let them back in. That's why I don't take them.

I need for there to be only one finger up and that's the one that says, "I don't want to do this anymore, I want to change."

I take one out of every twenty fellas. I'm not interested in wasting my time on someone who is not serious about changing, or in someone who I know will leave due to the family giving into their pressure.

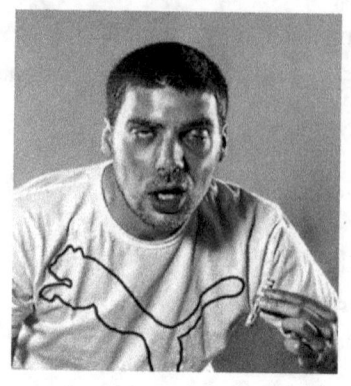

Tim

Hi, my name is Jim and my wife is Julie and we have 4 children, 3 boys and a girl. Three of our children are wonderful and cause no issues although our eldest, Tim, has had issues that became worse when he got his first part time job at 14. It started with marijuana with his mates, then alcohol, then prescription drugs. As he has ADHD and anxiety he seemed to think taking prescription drugs like Valium was okay. This increased and he then met a crowd that were occasionally smoking ice. This made him worse. We had him in a detox facility twice, trying to get him away from these so-called friends, but he just ends up back there. More recently he's taken some of our possessions and sold them for drugs.

This is breaking our heart and affecting the rest of the family. Deep down Tim is a polite and hardworking young man. He's just finished his third year as an apprentice at 21 years old but due to lack of work he's been put off. This has made him worse with the boredom. He moves out intermittently and comes home after a four or five-day binge. We have now told him he's not allowed back into the house until he gets proper help.

As I am a FIFO my wife is worried when I am away. We have been everywhere but there seems to be only counselling available but that's just not enough for Tim. He needs long-term rehab in an environment that's clean of drugs, phones, iPads & especially Facebook. We are at our wit's end; we love him dearly but feel soon Tim will either be in prison or just another statistic.

It would be interesting to unpack what is happening with Tim when he was 14, when he was an A. You can clearly see the progression from A to B then to C, D & E. When a person is an A, it's possible to be able to reason with them, to get them to look at the options that are available to them, as well as look at what is unfolding that causes them to make the decisions they are making. When a person has ADHD and anxiety issues and then use drugs like cannabis and meth, it gives them the confidence and boldness to fit where they never fitted before. They also find a whole new level of acceptance from their peers that they never had previously. All of a sudden, they are cool, or so they think.

I personally think it's a waste of time forcing a person to go into rehab when they don't want to go. You're wasting their time and the rehab's time as well as everyone involved. You're also putting them in with people who are serious about wanting to change and because of him not being serious about wanting to change, he destroys it for those who are, therefore taking other people out in the process.

Seriously, don't you think that if you can bring a person to the bottom of the bottom of the bottom, and when they're in that place, you give them instructions as to what they need to do that they would be more likely to reach out and grab what's offered. If they're just going because they had a bad batch of gear or you're telling them to, then it's a waste of time.

This family above is also a part of the problem. They learned the hard way like most families do. Sooner or later, things get to the point that the families won't let them into the home any longer because they know they are not qualified to help him.

What's sad is I know that the other children within the home would have been exposed to so much of their brother's stuff and it's in them, it's in their hearts and it changes who they are as people. You must act sooner, be strong. If this family knew half of what Tim had been up to, they would have had a heart attack.

Mandy's Brother

Hi, just wondering how/if you help those that are homeless and on drugs? Asking for advice also. My brother was living with myself and my husband and children as he got kicked out of his rental (owed rent, etc.) To make a long story short, he stole, lied to us and brought drugs into my house so have since kicked him out. He has depression and anger issues also. I tried helping him as I was all he had left. My parents and sister basically have disowned/can't deal with it or refused to help him or even to help me help him. He put my children in danger and they are now scared of him. He says he is no longer on drugs but I don't believe him.

He is now living in his car and says he goes to Woolies and walks around there so he can eat. I don't know what to do. I let him stay here, tried helping him, helped him get a car and some jobs doing gardening but he basically just ripped my heart out and stomped on it when he stole and lied. My husband and I have both told him to contact your organisation and others as well. He says he wants help but just keeps going the same way. We've actually had him reported to police as he came around after we discovered he had stolen from us and threatened me, my house, car and other threats. Denied that he stole, and kept denying. I asked him to come talk to me and own up and we'd try to sort it out before we got police involved, but he wouldn't. The police have found our items at Cash Converters.

My parents are divorced and not entirely on peaceful grounds with each other. My dad and brother have not ever had a good relationship due to my brother stealing from him a lot when my parents were together. My mum kind of always stuck up for my brother or "took his side". Sorry to go on but I'm stuck and any help would be great. Thank you (Mandy).

Through my eyes

What I'm going to do is break the above email down a little bit to walk you through some of what I see. You should be able to see what I see if you have read the first half of this book.

Just wondering how/if you help those that are homeless on drugs and so on? Asking for advice also. My brother was living with me and my husband and children as he got kicked out of his rental (owed rent, etc.)

"You bring a fully loaded meth addict into your home and you bring a world of evil with them."

This family would have known that something was not right before they brought him into their home or at least they would have had some idea. Drug addicts are extremely good at hiding the facts (you can see by the end of this email) that it had been an ongoing problem that had affected both Mum & Dad so she only has herself to blame thinking that she could do what

Mum, Dad and her sister could not. What scares me is that you bring a fully loaded meth addict into your home and you bring a world of evil with them. What's in them will spread to the rest of the people in your home, your children included.

To make a long story short, He stole, lied to us and brought drugs into my house so have since kicked him out. He has depression and anger issues also.

This is what drug addicts do and you should not be surprised at it. If they didn't that's when you should be surprised. The depression and anger issues are caused by the drug use as well as unresolved childhood issues.

He has been listening too much to the D voices and the D has deceived him and gotten entry into his heart – anger, bitterness, rage, unforgiveness, resentment and the list goes on.

I tried helping him as I was all he had left. My parents and sister basically have disowned/can't deal with it or refuse to help him or even to help me help him. He put my children in danger and they are now scared of him. He says he is no longer on drugs but I don't believe him.

He is now living in his car and says he goes to Woolies and walks around there so he can eat. I don't know what to do. I let him stay here, tried helping him, helped him get car and some jobs doing gardening but he basically just ripped my heart out and stomped on it when he stole and lied, etcetera. My husband and I have both told him to contact your organisation and others as well. He says he wants help but just keeps going the same way. We've actually had him reported to police as he came around after we discovered he had stolen from us and threatened me, my house, my car and other threats. Denied that he stole, and kept denying. I asked him to come talk with me, own up and we'd try to sort it out before we got police involved but he wouldn't. The police have found our items at Cash Converters.

You can tell clearly that the Mum, Dad and sister have learned the hard way. All of them have been taken out by him and now it's her turn, so sad. Here is another perfect example of a family who is destroyed by drug abuse, lies, deception, unforgiveness, division, resentment, deceit, betrayal and theft. She said above that her brother has put her children in danger but I honestly believe it's the other way around; she put her children in danger and fear has entered her children's hearts. She would have known what he was like and had some idea of what he had been up to. He had stolen from his Dad, the parents split up probably because of him, Mum tries to stick up for him and Dad says to kick him out and it gets worse, another family destroyed.

She is honestly not qualified to help her brother in the way that she wants to. What she needs to do, is to encourage him to make right choices. She can however do some research on his behalf but put the ball in his court; let him be the one to call around and make the appointments.

You will find most are not willing to go to rehab and how you tell that is you give them the numbers and tell them to call. You will find they will make two calls and say, "They have a three-month waiting list," or "They won't see me till Thursday," or "They say you're not allowed to smoke cigarettes,", they're not serious, they are just looking for a short-term fix until other options are available. If they were serious they would put a whole heap more effort in. If they were looking for drugs they would come up with the $100 to get the hit, but yet can't seem to get the fifty cents to make a phone call or the fuel to get to the appointment.

My parents are divorced and not entirely on peaceful grounds with each other. My dad and brother have not ever had a good relationship due to my brother stealing from him a lot when my parents were together and my Mum kind of always stuck up for my brother or "took his side". Sorry to go on but I'm stuck and any help would be great. Thank you (Mandy).

Can you see a glimpse of what I see? I see this all the time. I see it in its early stages, in the middle and like this. The parents' relationship is destroyed by his drug abuse and you're then continually handling it wrong and it's not right – PEOPLE, WAKE UP! Here is another perfect example of a family destroyed by drug abuse, lies, deception, unforgiveness, division, resentment, deceit, betrayal, theft.

How about we roll the clock back a bit before Mandy brought her brother into the house. She would have known the problems he was facing because of what her parents and sister went through. She would be up on all the issues and would have had an idea. What about if she did what I suggested above and chose to keep the lines of communication with him open, but from a distance?

When he rings up crying saying, "Sis, I need some help, I don't know what to do."

What she instead should say then is, "Brother, I'm not qualified to help you, but these people are," and then gave him a list of rehabilitation centres or counselling services and encourage him to make the call.

I know it's hard, but over time it works. He may not accept it the first time or the second or even the third but when he is ready he will. Most, if not all drug addicts, who come to you for help want help their way, they know how you need to help them and this is how you do it. Whatever you do don't do what they want you to do, but what they need you to do.

"One by one, they all become a victim of his choices because they failed to do what they knew in their hearts they must do."

In closing this story, Mandy deserves everything she gets for doing it the way that she did. She would have known in her heart that she is stupid for having him in the home, yet she went and did it anyway. Surely seeing what the rest of the family went through and what it did to them, she would have been aware of the risks, but she did it anyway. First his wife would have got knocked out, then Mum and Dad, then Brother and now the Sister... one by one, they all became victims of his choices because they failed to do what they knew in their hearts they must do.

Jay

Jay has been battling an 18-year addiction to drugs and substances, the chances of him just quitting cold turkey are few and far between. Don't get me wrong, some people do, but not many. When you have been using drugs for 18 years straight you can't just stop unless you learn a whole heap of new behaviour patterns.

There are different ways to process problems, ways to respond to people when you're confronted or when the pressures of life come your way. You need to deal with them differently rather than sticking a pick in your arm, popping a pill or downing a six pack of beer. A person with an addictive nature swaps one substance for another for another. They go from the beer to the speed, from the speed to the pot, from the pot to the pills, from the pills to the meth and the cycle continues. Unless they have some substance in their system that gives them a release from life and the stuff that comes with it, they don't know how to cope. They use drugs or substances to help them fit in or to feel normal.

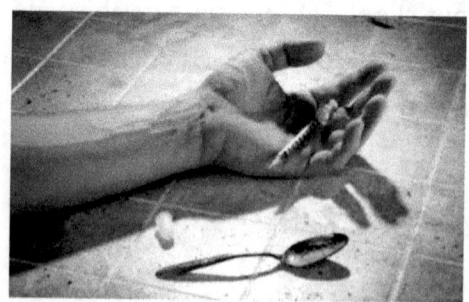

Hi, I'm just enquiring about your programme for my brother-in-law, Jay. He is 31 years old and has been struggling with a drug addiction. Yesterday it reached a crisis point when he was violent towards his partner in front of their two children. She has now left him and he will no doubt continue to seek more drugs as he goes on this downward

spiral. We have evidence that he has been using ice as well as marijuana. He also smokes cigarettes and drinks alcohol.

Jay has a beautiful heart but isn't himself. He has probably been battling addictions from around the age of 13. His parents don't know what to do. He has begged for money from them, as well as from his brothers. He comes from a big, supportive, loving family who all want to help him but don't know quite what to do. I came across your website and I think your facility would be great for him. Do you have any room available for him? And how could we get him into your programme? I'm worried he would resist any intervention but he clearly needs help. I look forward to hearing from you.

With someone like Jay, my personal opinion is that he will need a rehabilitation centre if he wants to kick drugs once and for all. It's not as easy as just stopping, especially with his history. When I take fellas into my programme we have a cold turkey approach to rehabilitation. We don't give them anything (always follow the doctor's recommendation). They have an addictive nature; why on earth do I want to take them off an illegal drug just to put them on a legal one?

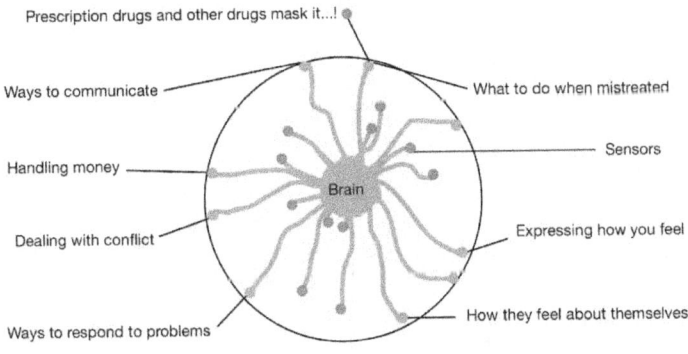

All my fellas do it cold turkey, except of course alcohol, and yes, that includes smokes.

Do you remember back in the day they used to have these electric plasma balls that had a force of energy on the centre and when you put your fingers to the outside of the ball all these static electricity bolts of lightning would touch the tips? Well that's a lot like our mind, when you take away the drug we need to hook all the senses back up again and that takes time. It's like the drugs put a force field around what we want to hook back up again so we get rid of it and plug them back in one by one, while at the same time cleaning up the heart.

TOUGH LOVE

CHAPTER ~5~

Desperate Families

Here are some requests from desperate families

Hi Peter, how does one get their Son into your programme? I am very concerned about my son. However, it's such a difficult one as I am aware that in most cases they have to be the ones willing to go into rehab on their own. My son has been into rehab, we made him go. Unfortunately, he did not complete the rehab as his baby was due in December. His wife and, of course, he himself wanted to be home for the birth. At the time, the rehab gave him the OK to go home and told me he was fine. I don't have proof that he was back on drugs, but from what his wife tells me and him not answering my phone calls or text messages, I'm certain his back on it. My Husband and I truly don't know what more to do. He's an adult and married with 3 children, we truly feel for his family. I don't know what to do anymore. His name is Fred (alias) his number is 0123 8765.

I'm a Mother crying out for help. Please try and call him, maybe he will listen to you. I have read your testimony and it touched me in such a big way. I follow you on Facebook and the work you doing is amazing. I honestly don't know what to do. This time he's got no contact with us. I feel for his innocent children aged 6 and 4 years, both boys and he's been blessed with a beautiful daughter on 8 January this year. He's not been home since Mother's Day as his wife put out a restraining order on him. I know he's angry about that, but I understand. Yes, at first, I thought how can his wife go to that extreme, but I had to understand I don't live with them and for a woman to do that she must have had reason. My husband refuses to believe my daughter-in-law. He won't speak to her and blames her that my son is in this position because she believes he must hit rock bottom. He's hit rock bottom already, but he has made these bad choices, not her. I have handed my son to God because I don't know what more to do. I'm stressed, I have cried a river, I am honestly a mother pleading for help. I don't know what more to do. But there's you and you got through this. Fred knows God yet he continues to turn his back on him. This is killing my husband and me. Please advise me Peter. Thank you, God. Bless you and your family and what you are doing.

I plan to break this down to tell you what I see:

Hi Peter, how does one get their Son into your programme? I am very concerned about my son. However, it's such a difficult one as I am aware that in most cases they have to be the ones willing to go into rehab on their own.

At this stage, it is mandatory that the person wanting the help must want it and must be willing to do it of their own accord. You can't force them.

My son has been into rehab, we made him go. Unfortunately, he did not complete the rehab as his baby was due in December. His wife and, of course, he himself wanted to be home for the birth.

It is extremely hard for co-dependant families to stick rehabilitation through. The wife wants the man home and the man wants to be at home. It takes a great deal of grunt and determination to stick it through. What generally happens is that he lasts a few months if he is lucky and on every visit, he tries to see if there is a gap in her stance on him having to be in rehab. As soon as he finds it, he's off back home.

At the time the rehab gave him the OK to go home and told me he was fine. I don't have proof that he was back on drugs, but from what his wife tells me and him not answering my phone calls or text messages, I'm certain his back on it. My Husband and I truly don't know what more to do. He's an adult and married with 3 children, we truly feel for his family. I don't know what to do anymore. His name is Fred (alias) his number is 0123 8765. I'm a Mother crying out for help. Please try and call him, maybe he will listen to you. I have read your testimony and it touched me in such a big way. I follow you on Facebook and the work you doing is amazing. I honestly don't know what to do. This time he's got no contact with us. I feel for his innocent children aged 6 and 4 years, both boys and he's been blessed with a beautiful daughter on 8 January this year. He's not been home since Mother's Day as his wife put out a restraining order on him. I know he's angry about that, but I understand. Yes, at first, I thought how can his wife go to that extreme, but I had to understand I don't live with them and for a woman to do that she must have had reason. My husband refuses to believe my daughter-in-law. He won't speak to her and blames her that my son is in this position because she believes he must hit rock bottom. He's hit rock bottom already, but he has made these bad choices, not her. I have handed my son to God because I don't know what more to do. I'm stressed, I have cried a river, I am honestly a mother pleading for help. I don't know what more to do. But there's you and you got through this. Fred knows God yet he continues to turn his back on him. This is killing my husband and me. Please advise me Peter. Thank you, God. Bless you and your family and what you are doing.

What I see here is a mother who has refused to let go of her son. He is a married man with three children who does not live at home and here Mum is putting her nose in where it does not belong. Some people might disagree, but unless he has asked for her input, she should really stay out of it and do her best to remain a neutral party.

One of the reasons she should stay out is also because of the drug. If you put your 20 cents in where he or she has not asked for it, then there is a possibility that he will take what you are doing or saying as a form of judgement. Even though they might not say it right there and then, they will think it. What the Mum needs to do is let go, stop wanting to know everything and set some boundaries like what I have listed previously at the start of this book. The parents here, as you can see, are controlling and would be a very big part of the problem. Even though they can't see it, they are. They think that they are doing and saying the right thing, but in fact are not. Again, you can see by the way the mum is putting in input as to what the wife should and should not do is also not okay. Sadly, the division that takes place among the family can destroy them as well as those they love.

IT'S POSSIBLE TO REPAIR THE DAMAGE TO THE FAMILY

Good morning, I'm desperately on a mission to help my husband. He's addicted to meth and he wants help but is finding it hard to take that step. He's never liked stepping out of his comfort zone on a normal day and I think the idea of being part of something like this is overwhelming. Would you be willing to come around and talk to him? I think if he was in his comfort zone and could meet that way it would help a lot. He's a good hardworking country boy at heart, very handy and a great leader when he's in his glory. Do you have a place for him if he was ready?

SOME COUPLE'S RELATIONSHIPS DON'T HAVE TO END, IF THEY WOULD ONLY JUST LISTEN

Hi, my son is 26 and has been alcoholic and now a drug addict. He has been on ice and anything he can get his hands on for 4-5 years. He has lost his home, partner and custody of his 5-year-old boy. Living at home on and off with us. Has lost his job twice, tried to commit suicide several times. The stress as parents is killing us. His Dad has just had major surgery for cancer and cannot take anymore. My son has had naltrexone implants put in by Fresh Start and they have not worked. I have now said that he has to choose between his family/home or drugs, we can't deal with it anymore. I believe he wants to get clean but has no faith in any treatment. If he wanted to get of the gear, how does he get onto your programme and what does it cost? I truly want my son back to his lovely self.

Hi Peter, I'm after a little help on behalf of a family friend. Their 26-year-old son has been using both marijuana and ice for some period of time and recently tried to commit suicide. He has recently been diagnosed with narcissistic personality disorder. He doesn't work, steals to support his habit and not even the birth of a child two years ago has helped with his choice of lifestyle. Attempts to get him into rehab or to stay in rehab haven't been successful. Even though his Mum has cut him off in every way possible, she still will listen to his abusive phone calls and like most Mums, only wants her son to be happy and well. I know you may receive hundreds of these emails a day, but your advice or help would so gladly be received....Thanking you .... Mel

Hello Peter,

My name is Ursula and I really need some advice. I know a phone call would be best, but I'm so emotional that I struggle to find the words.

My little brother turned 18 this year. He's been in a downward spiral for the past few years. He's always in trouble with the law, it started off as smoking pot and borrowing my dad's work car without my parents' knowledge and getting caught in speeding fines. And now he is using meth and just on Saturday had a knife to my dad's throat and threatened to stab him, all because he was bored and he wanted money which my parents refused. They had just paid off a drug debt for him and he came home wrecked the next day...

My parents are heartbroken and in total shock. My dad is a nervous wreck, they've had the police remove him and has a temporary restraining order on him but all the police did was give my parents a card and drop Brandon (my brother) off at some random's house. He's smashed his bedroom door in. His temper is insane. My mum is worried sick but now she fears for her life and my dad's as well and they no longer feel safe having him at home. Today he went to my parents' house and was banging on doors and windows. They were scared, so they called the police again and he was taken in and fined...

In the past, they've tried counselling and half the time he didn't show up. He's only lasted about a week in any job he's been given opportunity to. Including some family friends that gave him the benefit of the doubt but he decided one day he just didn't want to go.

He doesn't want to work. He has no money. He can't be bothered with Centrelink. He despises my parents and blames them for everything. It only came to light that he is using meth 2 weeks ago, however I only found out on Saturday. I don't know how long he's been using. At the moment, my family is terrified and are at their wit's end. And at the moment they feel like "...they just can't do it anymore".

I want to help him. I know he needs help. He's in such a dark place I'm worried he's going to hurt himself or someone else. He has often spoke of killing himself but now he is threatening other people. I don't know what to do or how to approach it. And at the moment he won't answer his phone so I can't speak to him.

He's so young, and I know he's probably feeling really alone and abandoned. He keeps making all these shitty life choices and the crowd he hangs around I don't have any faith in, obviously he's getting meth from someone.

If you could please give me some advice on how to approach things or even point me in the right direction of getting him help. I won't give up on him. I don't want to stuff things up by going about it the wrong way.... I'm his oldest sister, and he has always kind of looked up to me in the past.

I'm currently a FIFO worker on site so phone calls may be a bit hard as I'm only available after hours. But I really would appreciate anything you can tell me. Thank you for taking the time.

Hi Pete,

Can you please ring me ASAP regarding my 24-year-old son Gavin? Needs me to give him $600 so some bikies don't throw him off a balcony or shoot him - to pay for drugs. I don't want to enable him. He said he will talk to you about turning his life around, says he wants to change. I need wisdom. Any advice for me please?

My Damien is a chronic alcoholic with a wife who is battling breast cancer and 4 small children under 15. I have tried on numerous occasions to get him to rehab but he only did this once then doesn't go which causes him to relapse. This is causing great distress to loved ones. He drinks morning until night, every day. Damien is only 36 and we would appreciate your input or help. Hoping to hear from you. Please contact me anytime, heartbroken Mum.

My nephew is a gambler. It has taken its toll on my sister and her now separated husband. He has Tourette's and is on medication but this is his crutch. He lies and steals to support his habit. He is in his thirties. Is there any help we can get him and my sisters family? It's at breaking point now, kind regards,

Thank you, Sue

Hi Peter,

I have a son who has been addicted to alcohol and drugs for some time now. He is 38 years old. We have had many, many incidents and problems with his anger and behaviour including problems with the police.

He is a spray painter and works with his Dad in a family business. However, due to the current economic downturn, his constant bad behaviour, getting into all sorts of trouble, and also constant anger towards his Dad, the business has suffered tremendously. We never know when he is coming in to work or not and he sometime refuses to answer the door when his Dad goes around to pick him up for work. When at work he erupts, has a melt down with his Dad and then leaves. Leaving his Dad to carry on without a spray painter and trying to complete the work alone.

He has lost his driver's licence many times and has not held one for many years now. I also worry about him losing his house as he is always behind with his loan repayments and accounts. There is no way that he would be able to hold down another job because of his behaviour and my husband has tried very hard just kept the company going, trying to establish work for him in the future. And hoping that he would be stable enough to take over the business.

With my husband now at the point where he will have to close the business, and also the worry of something bad happening. I am looking for some sort or alternative, or help for my son. I would love for him to get into your programme, however, he does not think that he has a problem and constantly blames his father. He has been having some knee issues and will need an operation which is now booking in for February. He has his own home and we never know what state he may be in and he does not like us coming to his home unless he knows we are coming.

Hi there,

I'm not entirely sure where to start. My name is Brian and I'm a drug addict that's sick and tired of this endless cycle. My life as a drug addict has been like a constantly turning wheel that crushes all in its way.

In as little as 2 months I have spent roughly $30,000 (No there isn't an added zero, that is the estimated total sum) on synthetic marijuana. I smoke as little as 3g - 7g a day. It depends on my mood. I am currently on a CBO due to crimes committed to fund my drug addiction.

I have attempted detox/rehab within Victoria but I've always felt it's too close to home. Easy enough to leave and hitch back home. That's why a friend of mine sent me a link to your Shalom House, which claimed to be the "strictest rehab in Australia".

I was immediately drawn to your Rehab over others as you seem to actually take the time to help the addict.

I've applied to the Magistrate for permission to leave Victoria to attend your programme if I am eligible. I initially started as a regular cannabis user but that ended up not being enough so I hit the opium and morphine. From there I started experimenting with Angel Trumpets and other hallucinogens/deliriants (Mescaline, LSD, LSA).

Then I got hooked on the synthetic cannabis because I thought it wouldn't be as addictive....how wrong was I? Anyway, I think I've rambled on enough about myself.

Can you please help me change my life before I destroy myself and the ones I love?

Thanks for taking the time to read this message and hopefully I hear from you soon with some good news because I am currently standing on the gallows with a noose around my neck.

Hi Peter,

I appreciate your help. It is actually my husband Fred who I am talking about, who after 25 years married, we have just separated. Not my choice. Fred says he cannot continue to live a lie & has chosen not to continue walking with the Lord & is very much living an out of control life with very little sleep, drinking, clubbing & heavily into porn, excessive spending, inappropriate massages & "hooking up" with various women. He says he is a mess & needs to sort his life out, but not sure he is ready to let go just yet.

His bosses & workmates are all concerned for him too & told him to get help. He has so many people praying for him & for an opportunity for him to be free from his addictive & harmful behaviours (people don't know the sexual issues). He hates what all this is doing & the guilt eating him up, but has currently chosen to mask the problems.

He thinks there is no way out of the situation & obviously enjoys it at the time, but the guilt eats him up so much. I love my husband so much & know he is very sick mentally & truly believe he will come out the other side of this well. We also did not have any issues regarding intimacy & he would blame himself saying he just has no self-control. I really hope this or somewhere similar will be able to help Fred. Thank you!

Hi Peter, thank you for the newsletter, I am hoping you might be able to help my son. His name is Ray and he has asked me to please find someone to help him, as he is in a very fragile stage of his life. He has battled alcohol and pot since he was 15 years old. He has a heart of gold and will do anything to protect his family.

He has always worked as a brickie and worked hard. Ray suffers from anxiety and depression at times and has done so since he had Meningitis at the age of six. This has caused a huge amount of health problems with his eyesight and understanding of simple language.

Ray has had a massive scare in himself recently and needs help desperately. I was told about your programme and he really seemed to be very interested. He wants to change his ways and learn to deal better with his anger.

Would you please help him? I sent you his number yesterday on your phone, he might give up if he can't get help soon. I am worried as he is talking about us being better off if he wasn't here anymore and as a mother this is breaking my heart.

Dear Mr Lyndon-James

I am at a loss with how to help my son. Everything I do seems to make things worse. I would love for him to attend a programme like you offer but he thinks he does not have a problem with drugs, as I did when I was using and selling them.

I was sent to prison for 6 years, serving 4 before parole, just before he turned 14. That was the turning point for me leaving my children traumatised and to struggle on their own, and having our family home confiscated under the CPCA. I am hoping there is a way for James other than prison and before he has permanent brain damage.

James is now 20 years old and is smoking marijuana daily, occasionally using methamphetamines and MDMA and drinking. He was working for his brother who is a carpenter but eventually he started using drugs again and Wayne couldn't risk taking him on site under the influence. Since then he is continually being cut off Centrelink as he won't attend an appointment with his job search provider until he is cut off.

He is becoming more and more violent and abusive. I have called the police twice in the last month, the first time he hit his brother and the second he threatened to kill his sister. I have spoken to my counsellors, drug support line, Joondalup Mental Health but unless he will go willingly there is nothing they can do.

After walking down the street with a tomahawk one day, he finally agreed to go to Joondalup Mental Health. It took 3 months to get him there, then an hour and a half to get him from the carpark through the front doors, for less than 10 minutes with them. He came out with pamphlets for drug and alcohol counselling saying they said they could not help him.

He used to have days where we could talk rationally but there is no time anymore where he is not on drugs or coming down and he is becoming increasingly paranoid. I am so scared *for his safety and wellbeing as well as for the safety for his brother, sister and myself when he becomes irrational, violent and abusive.*

The police asked me last time if I would like to put a restraining order on him and I was torn with what to do. I don't want any harm to come to anyone because of his outbursts but I also don't want to harm him by pushing him away with nowhere but drug houses to go to.

Kind regards Jenny

Hi Pete I don't know which way to turn. My son needs help he has reached his lowest point. Someone is coming over this morning to pick him up but we have nowhere to drop him he has been on crystal meth but is off now but it's been a series of relapses. The police removed him last night but he turned up on my door step 2 o'clock this morning. Crying the drug has changed him. Will you take him? Someone can drop him off today. I am a Christian and have prayed for a way out, I know he is in good hands with you I have followed your story for a very long time and have seen the wonderful things you have done for these men. I am pleading with you to please take him in. I understand how busy you must be but I have no other option but to ask if you will take on one more. He used to be a beautiful young man but has lost everything.

Just say the word and we will drop him off.

Kindest Regards, Narell

TOUGH LOVE

CHAPTER ~6~

How To Get Your Loved One Back Again

IT'S POSSIBLE TO BRING THE OLD PERSON BACK AGAIN

A majority of the people I try to help are in a relationship, married or de facto. Sadly, the chances of them making it out the other side as a couple are very, very slim because many don't have what it takes and are not able to make the sacrifices to make it work. They are destined to fail because they are co-dependent and are not willing, unintentionally to do what it takes to make it work; well not in the way that they need to, but rather want to and that doesn't work. I write the following scenario as a warning to other couples who will read this book. I don't want your relationship to end.

Sometimes it takes a person on the outside to guide the two of you through a process until you can come out the other side. For a season, you need to allow someone to help you see what you can't see.

A tale of a typical drug addict and his story

Here is a married man in his mid-thirties with two children, aged three and seven. He has been with his wife for about eleven years. He has a previous history of drug use before their marriage and she stopped well before their first child was born. They are paying off their home and she is a stay-at-home mum. He has used meth on and off for the last couple of years that she knows of but recently it's come to the surface that it's been way more than she realised. She has confronted him many times over it and caught him out lying several times and no matter what, he keeps denying it. Financially the money seems to be disappearing, and she can't seem to prove where. She knows in her heart that he is using but can't get any proof.

He just continues to lie and make her feel bad for asking and confronting him, her heart is changing and she feels it. She knows that she needs to leave or kick him out but she thinks to herself, who's going to pay the bills, how do I pay school fees or what about the mortgage? Eventually, she has no other choice as it comes to a head and she kicks him out and seeks help from her parents to financially support herself.

His Dad and Mum step in for the short term by letting him stay with them while they try to work their differences out. In many cases the same lies and deceit take place. Meanwhile, they all discuss what the options are; rehabilitation or some form of counselling is put on the table. It's decided that it would be best if they undertake some form of counselling because if he went to rehab it would be too much of a strain on the family. They go for two or three visits and then he moves back into the home.

After another two visits, he decides it's not for him anymore and the commitment to go is gone. He goes okay for a month or two and the same stuff starts to happen again.

She senses things aren't right and then begins the same cycle all over again until this time, she kicks him out and says, "Unless you go to rehab you're not coming back here."

So he goes into a rehab and it lasts about three weeks. She sees signs of the old him coming back and starts to get a bit of hope back that things are going to be okay. She is struggling a bit at home with the kids and the money is very tight and she is doing it a little hard. When they talk on the phone, she downloads on him like she would normally, not knowing she is putting a weight on him.

Meanwhile, he is looking for cracks in her stance on him having to be in rehab, after all he is not there because he wants to but because she told him that he had to. Every time he talks with her, he looks for ways so that he can leave rehab and go home. Eventually, he sees a crack in her stance, he makes a whole heap of false promises and she gives in, he moves home.

They go good for about three months and slowly over time, he gets caught up again back up to his old tricks. She can tell he is using again and this times it ends really badly. She finds out that while he was on the gear he slept with another woman and he has spent all the savings, all his deception has come to the surface and a whole heap of what she didn't know is on the table. She gets brought to the point where she has no other choice but to move out herself back in with her Mum and Dad.

He starts to go into self-destruct mode and starts to go on long benders. While on these benders he starts to do things he regrets, makes calls that he shouldn't make and drops into see his partner when he shouldn't. Because of what's now taking place and his drug use his access to the children is limited unless he is under some sort of supervision and he starts to get angry.

One night he goes off and the police get called and he gets a restraining order put on him by the ex-partner and things go from bad to worse. Her heart is getting more and more damaged to the point she feels she could never trust him again no matter how hard she tries and she wants nothing more to do with him.

She starts to put things in place to protect her and the children and starts to think of a life without him. Things for him just continue to get worse. While all this is taking place he has been hitting the gear and who knows what else, feeling sorry for himself and going in self-destruct mode. The mortgage has not been getting paid and he has lost his job. His parents have tried to help financially but he has burnt them and spent the money on things he shouldn't. They realise that the money they have been giving him has gone on drugs. His brother and sister have helped out financially a couple of times but the same thing happens to them so they are reluctant to help any longer.

It gets that bad he ends up losing his house and has nowhere to go. It was suggested many times that he should go to a rehab, but he wasn't interested.

"I've tried rehab before," he said, "and it didn't work for me."

So as far as he is concerned, it's not an option. So, his Mum and Dad take him in because they feel sorry for him, they can't stand to see him on the street they say. He moves into Mum and Dads along with everything that's in him, the lies, deceit, anger, bitterness and unforgiveness. He is still using drugs and is out all night and sleeps all day. He's not doing his fair share around the home and is bumming off his parents.

He is really angry about what's been happening with his ex-partner and the kids, yelling and carrying on around the home all the time and making everyone in the house extremely uncomfortable and feeling like they have to tiptoe on eggshells around him.

He is blaming everyone else for what's happening including his parents.

"If you had brought me up different then I wouldn't be the way that I am", he says.

Mum and Dad allow some of his words to enter into their heart and they start thinking well, maybe it's true, that I am to blame or partly anyway.

They start to feel guilty, he can see it and uses it to his advantage. Mum and Dad start arguing with each other regularly. Dad says to do it one way and Mum says to do it another way. Mum tells Dad off for yelling at his son, Dad yells at Mum. Son argues back at Dad and the confrontation continues. People's hearts are changing, they can feel it. They don't want it to happen but it is, who they are as people is changing, they are getting a hardness in their hearts that was not there before, division is settling into the home.

His sister and brother have been telling Mum and Dad off for some time now for having him in the home and he has a go back at them. Now all the family are having a go at each other and the confrontation continues. It gets to the point that the parents can't handle it anymore and have to ask him to leave, but he won't go because he has nowhere else to go. Eventually he brings a whole heap of mates around one day and things get really bad. The parents have no choice but to call the police to have him removed. He yells at them and says a whole heap of bad stuff to dad, which leads to full-on confrontation and blows are exchanged. After that he is not allowed back at the home because of a move on order that was served by the police.

He goes on a destructive bender for a month or two and gets to a point where he is at the bottom of the bottom and rings Mum up crying saying, "Mum, I'm serious this time, I'm ready for change, I need help, I'll go to rehab, I'll do whatever you want, I'm ready for change."

Mum, in her stupidity, rings his brother and sister and says that she just heard from him and that he said he's ready for rehab. They think that now is their chance and they talked for some time and thought to themselves, "If only he would come to the point of wanting to change."

So, his brother goes and picks him up and takes him back to his house, and as soon as he gets there, they put him to bed so he can sleep. Then they all start ringing around getting the names and numbers of all rehabs, counselling services that deal with addiction and start making enquiries and appointments for the next day.

The next day comes and he can't get out of bed. He sleeps one day then two and then three and it moves into four, the only time he is out of bed is to go to the toilet or have a quick snack. Finally, on day four, he is moving around the house so they try to approach him about a couple of rehabs, half-heartedly he shows a little effort and attends one of the appointments but because they don't allow smoking it's not the one for him, so they try a few more. The next one is too far away and the one after that has too many lead up appointments and it seems too hard but he agrees just to keep the family happy. He sleeps another night and when he wakes up in the morning he says that he just has to duck up the road to pick up his phone, I won't be a sec he says, then four hours later he gets back.

You can tell he has been up to no good by the way he has all his energy back and by the way he is talking. You confront him and he does what he always does.

He turns it on you saying, "You don't trust me, no matter how hard I try you always have a go at me! Why should I try if you always do that to me?"

In the end, you have a big argument and he says stuff you and leaves. He blames you for why he is leaving and makes you feel like you stuffed it up even though he was the one that ducked off and got himself some drugs but you doubt now if you were right, even though you knew you were. So now he and his brother are not talking and the cycle continues again. He has just had a week's break off the gear thanks to his brother and he goes straight like a dog to the vomit and a pig to the mud.

All the family are angry at each other, one says we should have done it this way and another says we should be done it that way. More division, bitterness, anger and the cycle continues. He hits the drugs for another four months or so until one day he rings his sister up asking and begging for money. Apparently, he owes the bikies $2000 and if he doesn't pay it within 24 hours, it doubles to $4000 and another $2000 every other day. She panics and gives him the $2000 even though she knows she shouldn't. She didn't tell her husband or anyone else because she knew what they would say. Deep in her heart, she knows that she will never see the cash again.

Eight weeks later, it happens again. He rocks up at her doorstep, bloodied and bruised and crying, saying they are going to kill him. The bikies have given him 24 hours to come up with $10,000 or they have threatened to kill him and attack his family if he doesn't pay. She is in panic mode and doesn't know what to do so she rings Dad and he rings his other son and they start arguing again about what they should do or who should do what.

In the end, the sister is so scared for her brother that she pays the cash because he promised her if she did, he would go to rehab or do whatever it is that she asked from him. She pays the cash, then he disappears, because she paid the bills that took months to accumulate. Now he has no debt and he goes back like a dog to its vomit and a pig to the mud and the cycle continues.

Systematically one by one, each person gets taken out. His wife was first, his parents second, his brother third, his sister fourth, and fifth was Nan and Pop as well as a whole heap of his mates.

Now let's break it down

The above story is typical of nearly every meth addict, and I know that many people who read it will see themselves and what's happening in their lives at this present time and in what they have been through in dealing with a person on meth in that story.

I believe much of this can be avoided if only families would do things differently. What's frustrating for me is that I watch this as it all unfolds and can help them to prevent a lot of it, if only they would listen and allow me to speak into their life.

Sadly, they can't get their heads around not doing anything or can't seem to bear the thought that the loved one they care about is suffering and they think that by helping they are making a difference. But they are not helping at all as in most cases, it's making it worse depending on what stage of addiction they are in.

Like I said before I specialise in two things. The first is helping a person to change their life and the second is showing families how they can bring a person to a point where they want to change. Unless a person wants to change they never will, they will just do what they have to in order to get the outcome that gives them what they want.

> *"If you are dealing with a person on meth or other drugs, the earlier you can catch them out and put things in place to help them and you, the better."*

What I am going to do now is to pull apart the above story, tell you what I see and what I would do at certain times in the hope that you may be at that point right now and that you would be equipped to do what you are about to do differently. If you are dealing with a person on meth or other drugs, the earlier you can catch them out and put things in place to help them and you, the better. You don't have to get it wrong to get it right. It's best to listen to someone who has made the mistakes and learn from them. I know from my 26 years of doing drugs what people should have done to bring me and others to a point of wanting to change. I also know what to do because of what I do today in running Shalom House. I see the destruction meth and other drugs do to families on a daily basis and want to do whatever I can to help you to help others. I want to be there for you.

Okay, so here goes

Here is a married man in his mid-thirties with two children, aged three and seven. He has been with his wife for about eleven years. He has a previous history of drug use before their marriage and she stopped well before their first child was born.

A great deal of people have used drugs from an early age. Most start with cannabis as a social or recreational drug, as well as alcohol to fit in with mates or as a wind-down tool at the end of a hard day, or on weekends as a treat for working the week.

They consider it the standard norm.

"It's okay, everyone does it," they say and don't see any harm in it.

Over the years, they try other drugs every now and again like trips, ecstasy, speed and meth.

What is happening nowadays is that people think meth or ice is like pot. They think just because you can stick it in a pipe and smoke it that it's okay. Well, it's not. Yes, the stone that it gives you is different and more enjoyable than pot but the destruction it causes you and your home and the way that it grabs hold of you, is frightening. Many people, as they mature, stop using drugs, but there are also many who don't.

When you start to settle into a routine of married life and the years move on, things can sometimes get a little boring and you are tempted every now and again to try something different like it is with this fella. He works long hours during the week and has been mixing with a few mates at work and after a few beers one day smokes a pipe of meth. He finds out that he enjoys it and has a great night. Two weeks later after work the same thing happens again.

He has a few beers and one of his mates pull out a pipe, one voice says, "No, you don't need it," and the other voice says, "Go on, it's okay, everyone else is. You're not hurting anyone," and he chooses to listen to that one.

The thought that says, "It's okay, everyone else is doing it," goes from his head into his heart and it becomes his standard norm from then on, as a weekly thing. He accepts that it's okay. That's an A.

They are paying off their home and she is a stay-at-home mum. He has used meth on and off for the last couple of years that she knows of but recently it has come to the surface that it's been way more than she realised. She has confronted him many times over it before and caught him out lying several times and no matter what he keeps denying it. Financially the money seems to be disappearing and she can't seem to prove where.

One of the big hurdles for many families putting things in place for a person caught up in addiction, is the financial pressure they are under. Because there is already a strain on the finances due to his addiction, they can't just stop work and put him in somewhere for help. He would know he has a problem but has been hiding it from his wife for some time, too scared to speak up because of the consequences and also worried about what people may think. What he doesn't realise is the longer he keeps it in the dark, the further out of control his life will go, the harder it is to fix and the worse the consequences.

She has been seeing now for some time they have been under pressure by the lack of money in the bank and the number of bills building up. He has been lying to cover his tracks and dipping into the savings without her knowing, but it's getting harder and harder to hide. For the wife this is a strong indication that something is not right. Now if she looks for other signs to go along with this, she may be able to confront him sooner rather than later. A good way to know for sure is to get him to do a urine sample. Personally if I were the wife I would not be hesitant in confronting him and asking for a sample. She would have a strong gut feeling he was up to something because of the late nights and sleeping-all-day type symptoms on top of the financial ones.

You will find that when she confronts him and he can see that she is adamant about getting the sample, he will confess only to what he has to not to what he should, in order to relieve the pressure she is giving him. Whatever you do, still take the sample. You can't believe a word he says. You're not dealing with him, you're dealing with the drug.

He can't be trusted anymore and will only tell you what you want to hear not what you need to hear. As all this unfolds she really needs to protect her heart, otherwise she will change for the worse. Unforgiveness, resentment, anger and bitterness will enter her heart – she will feel betrayed and hurt. You need to look at an addict differently. They have a form of cancer. I'm trying to give you the cure and at the same time trying to protect you from being on the receiving end of its fruit. It really sucks on her end because of the violation she already feels from having to confront him, knowing that she is right yet he sits there and swears black 'n' blue that he is not up to anything. Personally, I feel like grabbing him by the scruff of the neck and banging his head against a wall.

If I were her, I would enlist the help of her (or his) parents at an early stage. Get a few people on board to help to keep him and you accountable and to help you to see what you can't. I would do it right from the start. I know you will feel a sense of shame or guilt, but push it off. Don't let it come on you as it will keep you in the darkness and you don't want that. Bring what's happening out into the light, so it will minimise its power over your life.

The more people you can get on board that you trust the better. Be careful of listening to everyone's opinions especially if they create division. Get him (with you) to a good counsellor and put things in place like urine tests to help you walk a straight path. Get him to approach the fellas he was getting the gear from and ask him to let them know he is struggling, that it's costing him his marriage and for a season put all control of the finances over to her.

Some people may say that I'm going too far with the suggestions that I have made, but I don't think so. I understand that every circumstance is different and in some cases you can't do all that I have said, but what you can do is your best and that's all that matters.

She knows in her heart that he is using but can't get any proof, he just continues to lie and make her feel bad for asking and confronting him, her heart is changing and she feels it.

When you confront a person and you know in your heart that you are right but yet can't seem to prove it; all they do is to continually deny it and plead dumb it hurts, you feel on the inside assaulted, hurt. You don't want to have to confront them, but you feel you must. You feel angry that they have put you in that position, you fire back at them and it brings out the worst in you.

"Know that you're not to blame and that you are doing what you need to do."

Most of the time when you do confront them, all they do is turn their back on you, making you feel like the one who has done wrong.

When you walk away after confronting them and couldn't prove anything, you start to get this voice, "Well, maybe you were wrong."

You start second guessing yourself and at the same time are really angry at them for putting you in this position. You are changing as a person, but you don't have to. Watch what thoughts you let into your mind, guard your heart. Try, yes try your hardest to keep calm and bring the truth or confront in love. Know that you're not to blame and that you are doing what you need to do. So what if you are wrong, it's better off being wrong than continuing on, not knowing for sure. Again a urine test can solve all this. Often a confronted person when backed into a corner will confess, but you must follow it through. If you are wrong, apologise.

Remember as I write about each section, that I am writing about where we are right now in the story and as if you hadn't done what I have suggested prior. What I'm trying to do, is to give you counsel as this unfolds. In the hope that if you are right now personally, at any particular point yourself, like where we are in this story, and then what I have written will help you to do what you need to do.

She knows that she needs to leave or kick him out but she thinks to herself, who's going to pay the bills, how do I pay school fees or what about the mortgage? Eventually she has no other choice as it comes to a head and she kicks him out in the meantime seeking help from her parents to financially support herself.

She has tried time and time again to try and find out what's happening but every time she asks all she gets is lies and denial. He hasn't been coming home until all hours in the morning and continues to make up stories as to where he has been.

She needs a break and feels that she should kick him out but then thinks how on earth can she pay the bills? She doesn't want to leave him. All she wants is for him to be honest, tell the truth and accept the help to change.

In the end she feels that she must leave him or kick him out until he can come clean and do things to change. Maybe this will be enough to force his hand and accept some help. She has threatened on many occasions to kick him out or go before, but because of what is unfolding she has no other choice, so she kicks him out. This forces her hand now to have to talk her Mum and Dad about what's been going on. For a long time she had been hiding it from them. They had an idea but now it's all out in the open. She tells mum and dad the whole story in order to see if they can help her financially for the short term, until she can get back on her feet or until they can works things out. The decision is made and she kicks him out.

Drug Test Kit

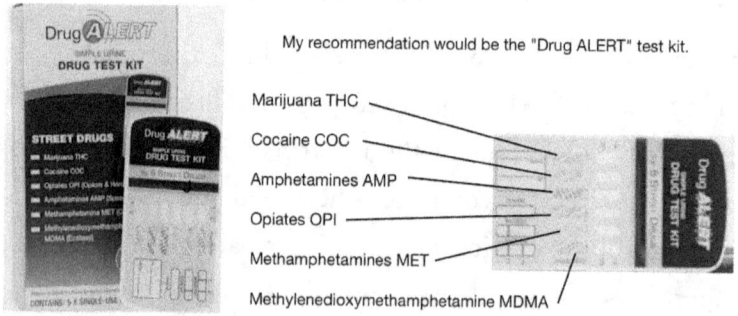

My recommendation would be the "Drug ALERT" test kit.

Marijuana THC
Cocaine COC
Amphetamines AMP
Opiates OPI
Methamphetamines MET
Methylenedioxymethamphetamine MDMA

One of the things I try to encourage is for families not to pass judgment or put their two bobs worth in. Rather come alongside the couple helping them to make right choices that over time will lead to the restoration of their relationship.

Parents tend to take sides, especially when it's in regards to their children. I'm sorry, but I feel the older generation does this more than most, as drugs and behaviour like this that has to do with drugs, to them, should not be taking place.

Personally again, if a urine sample had been taken a whole heap of boundaries should have been put in place like I suggested previously, but now that she has kicked him out, she needs to come up with a plan. Counselling and Rehabilitation Centres are on the table. I do not believe the two of them would be able to last the distance with him in a rehabilitation centre. Many people actually do need one, but not many people have what it takes to be able to do it unless their circumstances bring them to a point where they really want to or they have no other choice.

When they ring around the various rehabs asking about the programme, costs etc., they get put off by what the place does or does not offer, so they eventually settle for counselling. This is a good thing, as long as it complements certain boundaries that help to keep him on the straight and narrow and also holds him accountable. Counselling, along with urine tests, and controlled finances are always a great support for those who are struggling in addiction, even though at times they can be painful.

His Dad and Mum step in for the short term by letting him stay with them while they try to work their differences out. In many cases, the same lies and deceit take place.

Mum and Dad seem to be the ones who always step up to try to help their children. Their inexperience with drugs, lack of knowledge of it, and ability to detect them or the affects they have on a person already, start them off with a handicap when it comes to assisting him.

No family member should automatically just bring a drug addict into their home, without first establishing the boundaries. I don't think that's unreasonable, as you are not dealing with a person any longer, you are dealing with a drug. Personally I would draft up a few non-negotiable rules and before I allowed he (or she) into my home I would make sure they agreed to them, otherwise you are opening yourself up to a whole heap of problems.

These are some of the things that I would put in place:

- They must agree there is to be no using of drugs on or off the property while they are staying with you.
- Agree also that they will not bring drugs on the property or bring people who use them to the property ever.
- They must agree to attend some form of counselling.
- Also agree to undertake or be subjected to random urine testing where and when required, especially at random.
- Return home on a nightly basis and let you know if they are not going to and if they are not going to come home, where they will be staying.
- It's always a good idea to get them to pay towards rent and food and bills to do with their lodging.
- Make sure that they do their share of the chores around the home such as wash, cook and clean.

- Get them to make sure that they will never bring anyone to the property without permission.

- They should agree that there must be some level of transparency. You need to be given the right to ask questions at any time without the backlash of words like, "You don't trust me." Trust is something they must over time earn back.

- Establish a review time where they can review the agreement that was put in place before he came to stay. The first time should be after a week, then adjust where required. The second another week after that then as you feel comfortable with how things are progressing you can make it less frequent.

- The two parties should also put in place an exit strategy in case it doesn't work. Something where if one party feels that it's not going to work out then they have the others permission to back out, without either party taking offence.

- Try to identify the problems that you are going to come up against and how you are going to deal with them if they do, think ahead. If you can come up with the consequences prior and the two parties agree, then it makes it much easier to enforce.

Many families fail in discussing or communicating this before they allow their child into the home. What it does is puts the parents in a position where they are on the back foot right from the start. No time limit has been discussed or boundaries have been set, so when he doesn't pay his way or do his fair share of the chores, they start to hold offence. He doesn't come home for a day or two, or when he does he brings all these shady fellas with him and they leave you a little worried.

All of a sudden, you have no privacy any longer and you can feel the level of peace and security you once had in your home, has now gone. If a person put all what I have suggested in place above and both parties agree, you have established a good base in which to help him, while at the same time protecting yourself and those who live in your home from certain destruction.

> *"Your responsibility to look after them and provide for them stopped when they became grown men or women. They are adults and are responsible for their own choices now."*

Sometimes a person will challenge that and say you are being unfair, but you're not, it's your home they are entering. You know what boundaries you need in place for your home to function in the best interest of all concerned. Your responsibility to look after them and provide for them stopped when they became grown men or women. They are adults and are responsible for their own choices now. They are coming to stay at your home where you pay the bills and where you live your life.

They must understand you are about to make massive sacrifices to have them in your home and need to respect what you need to put in place to make your home function the way you want it to.

Meanwhile they all discuss what the options are; rehabilitation or some form of counselling is put on the table. It's decided that it would be best if they undertake some form of counselling because if he went to rehab it would be too much of a strain on the family. They go for two or three visits and then he moves back in home. After another two visits he decides it's not for him anymore and the commitment to go is gone.

Like I said before most families will use rehab as a last ditch option and nearly always go for counselling. Counselling is really only good if the person wants it and is willing to engage. If they are going because you are forcing them then I doubt very much they will get much from it, unless they open up and take it seriously. In a lot of cases that I have come across since running Shalom House and in my own life is they only go for as long as it takes for them to get back what they lost, and in this case, it's his wife and children. He goes for a few months until his partner weakens due to the stress they are putting on both lots of parents and thinks they should be able to do this together and she allows him back. Wrong move. Unless again some working agreement can be put in place that would ensure he continues on the paths of change that he has started, she should not bring him home – a bit like the one that's listed above.

He goes okay for a month or two and the same stuff starts to happen again, she senses things aren't right and then begins the same cycle all over again until this time she kicks him out and says "Unless you go to rehab you're not coming back here."

So he goes into a rehab and it lasts about three weeks. She sees signs of the old him coming back and starts to get a bit of hope back that things are going to be ok. She is struggling a bit at home with the kids and the money is very tight and she is doing it a little hard. When they talk on the phone she downloads on him like she would normally, not knowing she is putting a weight on him. Meanwhile he is looking for cracks in her stance on him having to be in rehab, after all he is not there because he wants to but because she told him that he had to.

Every time he talks with her he looks for ways so that he can leave rehab and go home. Eventually he sees a crack in her stance, he makes a whole heap of false promises and she gives in, he moves home.

I'm sorry to sound so cynical, but this is to be expected. You can't change 18 years of addiction to drugs with three counselling sessions, I mean, hello! Of course, it goes back to how things used to be. So sooner or later things come to a head again and she has kicked him out. This time rehab is the answer but the only reason he has to go is because she is telling him to. He is not going because he wants to, but because he has to and that's a waste of time.

What she should have done is not say, "Unless you get rehab, I'm not taking you back."

She should have just kicked him out and said, "Until you change there is no you and me."

Following that, she should prepare herself for a long journey ahead. She needs to bed down and restructure her life in a way that she can maintain it for the long term. If that means going back to work, changing the kids' schools, then so be it. Whatever has to happen to make it all work, she needs to do it. A large majority of people are not willing to make those sacrifices. They try to find an easier way to do it and at the same time trying to hold on to their lifestyle, but it doesn't work that way.

Most women, if they are a stay-at-home mum, can't afford to do what's required and stay in the home. Normally the women would have to move out to her parents or another family member's house because they can't afford to pay the mortgage or all the bills at home. Depending on how bad it got at home, they have no choice. Either way, no matter how financially well off they are (or aren't), they need to get prepared for the long journey ahead. For some ladies, they actually find it a relief that he is not in the home. A good example of what they have been through would be like they have been in the back seat of a car going 400 miles an hour with no control over anything, smashing into everything and not knowing how to stop. Well finally the ride is over, no more tiptoeing on eggshells, fresh air....

One of the keys to get through this is to know this may not be forever, but it will be for a while. Your mind is going to throw all types of things at you, watch what you think about. She needs to be set up in a way that she can look after herself until he is well again, at the same time protecting herself and the children from the consequences of his choices, as best as possible. This is not forever. When able to look after herself, hopefully positioning him to a point of reaching out for help because he wants to, not just because he has to.

I would encourage her to set a few boundaries with him and not to close all lines of communication. Keep them open and civil.

A couple of those boundaries might be:

- Don't let him stay over the night.

- Give yourself at least 4 weeks "you" time; have a break, refresh.

- Always meet with him in a public place, this will help you to stay strong and not to give into his manipulation.

- Reassure him that the separation is not forever, but that he must do things to change.

- Don't force him to do anything but encourage him.

Again, settle down and to the best of your ability get yourself ready for a long haul. He will know what he needs to do and who he should see. I don't believe you should spell it out for him, as he will only be doing what you have said to tick a box, because that's what you said. I believe that you need to do whatever has to happen to encourage his mind to think on its own accord what it needs to do.

They go good for about three months and slowly over time he gets caught up again back up to his old tricks. She can tell he is using again and this times it ends really badly. She finds out that while he was on the gear he slept with another woman and he has spent all the savings, all his deception has come to the surface and a whole heap of what she didn't know is on the table. She gets brought to the point where she has no other choice but to move out herself back in with her Mum and Dad.

As I write this I need to continually remind myself that I am writing this as if I have written nothing previously and that this is the point that she is about to act. So I don't just write this to remind me, but the reader also. I want to be able to put this down in such a way that if you're at this point now, then you can start here.

Well it's taken a long time but it's all come to a head and she knows that she has no other choice now herself, except to leave. She can't stay in the house any longer because she knows that she can't afford it. His drug use and the continued disruption to their cash supply and the mounting unpaid bills have now made it a certainty. Not to mention her finding out that he had been unfaithful, for the first time she knows of, anyway.

When a person goes through this level of lies and deceit for a long period of time, it continues over time to change them into a person they never dreamed of being. She would be going through thoughts about, is she good enough, has she done something wrong, or could she have done something differently. Not to mention the thought like, I never thought that I would be a single mum; what about the children growing up without their Dad and what will people think of me? It shows a great deal of hurt, resentment, bitterness and anger in the heart. She doesn't want it there but it enters her heart and what's inside her operates through her and overtime changing her as a person. Many women carry that into the next relationship and when they get through the butterfly experience of falling in love again, all the distrust comes to the surface and the new relationship struggles, unless it's dealt with. When a relationship breakdown gets to this point, it takes a great deal to save it.

Somehow the guy really needs to come to the point where he hits the wall and hits it hard. He needs to come to the point of wanting to change because he wants to, not because she wants him to. He needs to come to the point where he is doing it for him. You would be surprised how many men say to me they want to come to rehab, so that they can get their children back or their wife back. I know that you may think this is wrong but that's the wrong reason. You need to want to do it for you, because you've had enough and you want to change.

My advice to her at this point is to do what you can now, to get you and your children settled for the long haul. Deal with what comes your way the best way that you can. Be wise in paying certain bills as every dollar will count for the short term. Be prepared to have to go bankrupt as your name is on half the bills and there will be no way he will be paying them.

I can say that for sure unless he wins a heap of money, or Mum and Dad want to pour it down the drain and pay it on his behalf. That's what a lot of parents do before it gets this bad. They pay loans and mortgage payments, lend money not knowing that all they are doing is feeding his or her habit.

I would strongly suggest that she see a counsellor if she hasn't or isn't already. There will be a lot for her to go through and she shouldn't do it on her own. Try your best not to listen to everyone bad-mouthing him or telling you what they think you should do, as it's not helpful to you or your long term relationship with him as the children's father, regardless of how it all turns out.

He starts to go into self-destruct mode and starts to go on long benders. While on these benders he starts to do things he regrets, makes calls that he shouldn't make and drops into see his partner when he shouldn't. Because of what's now taking place and his drug use his access to the children is limited unless he is under some sort of supervision and he starts to get angry.

He knows it's the end of the line now and goes into panic mode trying to hide the reality of where he is at and what he is facing. He has no job, has lost his wife and children, and this time it looks like it's for good as she knows he cheated on her. He has people ringing him for outstanding bills and can't get enough money to support his habit. He has been selling and swapping assets to get by.

He is thinking to himself, "Stuff it, I've lost everything – I might as well hit it hard," and so he does.

While off his face, he tries to ring his ex and it all goes south on him, he starts to yell at her and make threats and she responds back. It's not good. She starts to think he is not good for the children and starts to set boundaries that he is not in a position to accept because of his mental state. He can't seem to see it's not just for him but also for the children, no matter how it's presented. He just sees it as an attack and thinks that everyone is against him.

> **"Remember that you are dealing with the drug and not the person...ice users do not see common sense very easily when they are off their faces."**

If I were her or any family member, the less you say is the more you say. For your sake and his, try not to communicate with him when he is in a worked up state.

Tell him in a nice way, "I don't want to hurt you or disrespect you or get on the wrong side of you, but I don't want to talk about it today while you are like this – please don't take it the wrong way."

Say something like that, but calmly and remember to guard your heart. Don't respond to the way that he is and try not to let him get to you. The only way you will be able to communicate any common sense to him is just after he has woken up after a good sleep. I personally think you are wasting your time and risking confrontation which you should try to avoid at all costs – it's not worth it. Remember that you are dealing with the drug and not the person. I am not trying to exonerate the person from the responsibly of their choices but rather help you to see you must do it differently. Ice users do not see common sense very easily when they are off their faces, most of the time what you say to them comes as an attack. Another protection measure I would suggest for the wife is to nominate a third party to do all her communication for her with him. I know that he won't like it, but for her and the children's sake, for the short term, it's the best way.

One night he goes off and the police get called and he gets a restraining order put on him by the ex-partner and things go from bad to worse. Her heart is getting more and more damaged to the point she feels she could never trust him again no matter how hard she tries and she wants nothing more to do with him. She starts to put things in place to protect her and the children and starts to think of a life without him. Things for him just continue to get worse.

Remember I am writing this as if I have written nothing previously. Because she failed to put boundaries in place, allowed him to continue to contact her and approach her, it's been escalating to the point where he knows that she is serious. There is no sign of her giving in to him and he is not prepared to take no for an answer. They have a huge argument and he throws her towards a wall and physically assaults her. Someone else steps in and there is a big fight. The police get called and he gets arrested. She knows that she has no other choice but to put things in place to protect her and the children, so she gets a restraining order. Now the thought of ever going back to him scares her. She knows in heart that it will never be the same again.

There are many times throughout this story where these things could have been avoided if people had done things differently and a lot sooner, but sadly they didn't because their emotions and co-dependency got in the way. People often call the counsel that I give them tough love, but I reckon that's a whole lot of hogley pop, a load of horse poo, a crack of dust; if you know what I mean. It's not tough love, it's cause and effect.

Here's an example.

You want to touch the hot plate and go to do it. I will stop you and tell you that you will burn yourself. You try to do it the second time. I might try to warn you again, but the third time, go ahead burn yourself now. You'll learn not to do that again.

"We should never spare the rod from our children, because that's how they learn." (Proverbs 13:24)

For crying out loud, parents, he is a grown man who by his own free will is choosing to stick battery acid in his lungs or veins. Any person in their right mind would know that there is a consequence to that and that's the chance you take. You don't just get high; you slowly deprive your family of a husband, a father a son and a best mate. Over time you lose your health and your mental state of mind.

While all this is taking place he has been hitting the gear and who knows what else. He is feeling sorry for himself and going in self-destruct mode. The mortgage has not been getting paid, he has lost his job. His parents have tried to help financially, but he has burnt them and spent the money on things he shouldn't everyone is running around frantically trying to save and move what they can. They eventually realise that the money they have been giving him, was spent on drugs. His brother and sister have helped out financially a couple of times but the same thing happens to them, so they are reluctant to help any longer. The whole family is taken back by the amount of lies and deceit that has been uncovered.

"Remember that change is only a choice away and that NO-ONE can change him, but him. He is where he is because of his choices."

Right now, this fella couldn't get much lower. He has lost everything and nearly everyone. No-one trusts him anymore and everyone knows that whatever comes out of his mouth is baloney. He hasn't seen his kids in a while because he is too embarrassed at how far he has fallen.

Financially he has no place left to bludge money from, as he has burnt everyone he knows. What I suggest to families here is that they should maintain strict boundaries when dealing with him. As hard as it is to see him like this; don't do anything for him, don't give him any money, don't tell him what you see, don't give him your opinion, don't do anything except be ready to encourage him to make right choices. Remember that change is only a choice away and that NO-ONE can change him but him. He is where he is because of his choices. I am not saying you give up on him but rather ALWAYS be ready to encourage him in making right choices but at the same time set your boundaries. Like what I have said many times over in this book;

Following is what I suggest to families to send by SMS or say verbally when the loved one calls asking for help.

(Name)..... you know that I love you and always will but I'm not qualified to help you. I am not going to be there for you in the way that you want me to but rather in the way that I need to. You are a grown man/woman now and are responsible for your choices. You need help and unless you seek the help and follow it through to the end, your life will not change. I am always happy to buy you a meal but I will never give you money or pay any of your bills or do anything for you, until you start to take the first steps. Here is a list of rehabs that I know can help you, pick one and get your life sorted out.

Then you pass him the list of rehabs. (Then include a list of rehabilitation or counselling support services for the person to contact relevant to the state or territory that you live in.)

It gets that bad he ends up losing his house and has nowhere to go. It was suggested many times that he should go to a rehab, but he wasn't interested. "I've tried rehab before", he said, "and it didn't work for me." So as far as he is concerned, it's not an option. So his Mum and Dad take him in because they feel sorry for him, they can't stand to see him on the street they say. So he moves into Mum and Dads along with everything that's in him, the lies, deceit, anger, bitterness and unforgiveness. He is still using drugs and is out all night and sleeps all day. He's not doing his fair share around the home and is bumming off his parents. He is really angry about what's been happening with his ex-wife and the kids, yelling and carrying on around the home all the time and making everyone in the house extremely uncomfortable and feeling like they have to tiptoe on eggshells around him.

He is blaming everyone else for what's happening including his parents. "If you had brought me up different then I wouldn't be the way that I am," he says.

Mum and Dad allow some his words to enter into their heart and they start thinking well, maybe it's true, that I am to blame or partly anyway. They start to feel guilty, he can see it and uses it to his advantage. Mum and Dad start arguing with each other regularly. Dad says to do it one way and Mum says to do it another way. Mum tells Dad off for yelling at his son, Dad yells at Mum. Son argues back at Dad and the confrontation continues.

People's hearts are changing, they can feel it. They don't want it to happen but it is, who they are as people is changing, they are getting a hardness in their hearts that was not there before, division is settling into the home.

Finally he has lost the home and is on the streets. Sooner or later he gets tired of couch surfing and is looking for a place to stay. Mum and Dad haven't heard from him for months and have only heard rumours of what's been going on. Then one day out of the blue they get a call. He begs and pleads with Mum to be able to stay just for a few days. She knows she shouldn't, Dad and her have a big argument. Dad feels bad and gives in, even though he knows that he shouldn't. They didn't set any boundaries other than make him agree that he would get help and he did, but didn't follow it through. The same deal goes here as before. Why on earth would you bring him into your home with all that's in him? Nothing has changed except he is homeless and has nothing, sure you feel sorry for him.

What they should have done before is NOT let him into the home. Like I said before say, "Son, you know that I love you and always will, but I'm not qualified to help you. I am not going to be there for you in the way that you want me to, but rather in the way that I need to. You are a grown man now and are responsible for your choices. You need help and unless you seek the help and follow it through to the end, your life will not change.

I am always happy to buy you a meal but I will never give you money or pay any of your bills or do anything for you until you start to take the first steps. Here is a list of rehabs and places that I know can help you, pick one and get your life sorted out."

Then you pass him the list of rehabs and counsellors. Tell him that he can NOT stay here; you DON'T let him into your home. He is past that point, even if you tried to put the boundaries in place like urine testing and things like no going out. It won't work as he won't be able to do it, you will be setting yourself up for a fall. The amount of crap that is in his heart that needs to be cleaned up, is huge. What they should do now is **GET HIM OUT OF THE HOUSE ASAP.**

Families make the mistake by bringing him in the house, only to lose their own marriages and relationships over it. Not only that, but by bringing him into the house you are affecting all the other people in your home. My gosh, how crazy are you? I also recommend when making a decision like that, all the family should come together and have a meeting. It should be discussed as a family and if everyone is not in agreement, then it should not happen and if they are, "set boundaries". Most families find by bringing him in the house that the house is no longer theirs, because he rules the roost. I hate roosters.

"Meth turns a kind man into a man full of deadly evil. It's not him anymore it's the drug."

Meth turns a kind man into a man full of deadly evil. It's not him anymore it's the drug. He changes the atmosphere in the house where everyone has to tiptoe around him just so they don't set him off. Mum, Dad, brother and sister all become scared of him because he is so unpredictable and can go off at the smallest thing. His brother and sister are concerned for the parents and have warned them many times not to let him in, as it's brought massive amounts of division among the family. So they haven't talked with Mum and Dad for a while, as it just ends in an argument all the time.

In the meantime, while he is in the home, what is in him is operating through him. He verbally assaults Mum and Dad on a daily basis saying all kinds of crap to his parents, wearing them down with his words. The parents take a lot of what he says to heart and start feeling partly responsible for why he is like he is. They start to feel an obligation to help him, because of all the guilt trips he puts on them.

His sister and brother have been telling Mum and Dad off for some time now for having him in the home and he has a go back at them. Now all the family are having a go at each other and the confrontation continues. It gets to the point that the parents can't handle it anymore and have to ask him to leave, but he won't go because he has nowhere else to go.

Eventually he brings a whole heap of mates around one day and things get really bad. The parents have no choice but to call the police to have him removed. He yells at them and says a whole heap of bad stuff to dad, which leads to full-on confrontation and blows are exchanged. After that he is not allowed back at the home because of a move on order that was served by the police.

By this time the parents have tried many times to get him to leave, but no matter what they do he won't and he continues to rock up regardless of what they say or do. The rest of the family have confronted him on more than one occasion and all he does for the short term is make himself scarce. One day when it comes to a head, as it will, it nearly always comes up with confrontation, which you should avoid at all costs.

The best way to get a person removed from the home is to get the family together as a group way before it comes to the police being called or to the point where something happens to force your hand. In this case it's Mum, Dad, brother and sister. When he wakes up one morning just after a shower ask him to sit and talk for a second before he leaves the home, have the brother and sister walk in around the same time and talk to him as a unified group. Say something like this;

"We don't want to hurt you or disrespect you or do anything that gets on the wrong side of you and we want you to know that we really care about you. We are not going to help you the way that you want us to but in the way we need to. You might not agree with what we feel we must do but we have thought long and hard about it. Mum and Dad are really struggling with you being here and they understand that you have no place to go, but they are not in a position to help you.

You need to attend some sort of rehabilitation centre or a counselling service to help you, because we can't. It's too much for us as they are getting taken out in the process. They can't do it anymore."

By then he will probably be yelling and carrying on but you must stay calm and communicate in love. You must in the best possible way get him to leave the home with as much minimum confrontation as possible. It's important that when he leaves that he must take all his gear otherwise it will just give him excuses to continue to come back. In this case the parents are not strong enough to say no to him. So if you can't get him to take his gear there and then you must move it to someone's house who is strong enough to stand up to him and not put up with his crap. You will find that he will find somewhere to move it to pretty quickly.

Remember you are dealing with years of addiction and he honestly needs a place that is equipped to help people like him. However unless he comes to that place where he is willing to do whatever it takes to change his life, then you are wasting your time.

Because no-one acted before it came to a point of conflict the inevitable unfolds, police and a restraining order is served. Now mum and dad have their home back and try to go in recovery mode, hurt, bruised and broken by what they have just been though. They are in a much worse of state than they've ever been in before. It is sad watching all this unfold and it can be prevented, yes, "It can be prevented if families stood up and did what they knew they should have done a lot sooner."

He goes on a destructive bender for a month or two and gets to a point where he is at the bottom of the bottom and rings Mum up crying saying, "Mum I'm serious this time, I'm ready for change, I need help, I'll go to rehab I'll do whatever you want, I'm ready for change."

Mum, in her stupidity, rings his brother and sister and says that she just heard from him and that he said he's ready for rehab. They think that now is their chance and they talked for some time and thought to themselves, "If only he would come to the point of wanting to change."

So, his brother goes and picks him up and takes him back to his house, as soon as he gets there they put him to bed so he can sleep then they all start ringing around getting the names and numbers of all rehabs, counselling services that deal with addiction and start making enquiries and appointments for the next day.

Remember I am writing this as if I have written nothing previously. I get many people at this stage; the fella is an E, right where you want him. He's at the bottom and what you do from here is very important. The LAST thing you do is let him into your home. No, don't do that, whatever you do DO NOT let him into your home, but sadly many people do. You need to leave him out on the street, you need him there, and you need him at the bottom. You're not qualified to help him, well not in the way you want to anyway. Please don't bring him into the home; it's taken a long time to get to this point.

What needs to take place is all those who he may ring, when he is at the bottom, should have come together by now as a group, nominated a group spokesperson or leader. One who is strong enough to stand up to him, one who will call the shots and one that everyone needs to go back to, in order to keep informed of what's taking place before they make any decisions.

Everyone must be prepared for the call that will be coming from him when he hits the bottom. Someone will get the call and when they do, regardless of who they are, they must all be prepared to do and say the same thing, taking advice from the leader. This is what you do when he rings up crying, you say:

(Name)..... you know that I love you and always will but I'm not qualified to help you. I am not going to be there for you in the way that you want me to but rather in the way that I need to. You are a grown man now and are responsible for your choices. You need help and unless you seek the help and follow it through to the end you cannot come back here. I am always happy to buy you a meal but I will never give you money or pay any of your bills or do anything for you until you start to take the first steps. Here is a list of rehabs that I know can help you, pick one and get your life sorted out. Then you text him a list of places that can help him, don't direct him to one particular one but let him make that choice. All rehabilitation centres are doing the best with what they have learnt and each one does it different.

Even though he has said all the right things like, "I'll go to rehab, I'll do whatever you ask," you still DO NOT let him into your home.

No, I'm sorry, not even for one night, because once you get him in your home, you are going to have a real big problem on your hands trying to get him to leave as well as many other problems. Remember, what happened to Mum and Dad, well that will happen to you.

At the moment, his brain is thinking, "I can't do this anymore."

What we need to do now is get the seed into his heart of, "I want to change."

How we do that is to leave him on the streets and encourage him to make the call. When people ring me needing help, I can tell if the seed is in the heart. I can water that seed and I know how to make it grow. When they ring me and it's there, I can tell. That's where I want them.

Pre-intake Checklist

Some of the things that I take into consideration before I take a person include;

- Are all the family on the same page and is one of the family going to shipwreck their rehabilitation by letting him come home early?

Unless everyone is all on the same page and are at the point of agreeing that under no circumstance will they take their loved one back until the programme has been completed, the chances of me taking the person in is slim. You would be amazed at how many families have allowed the addict to come back home

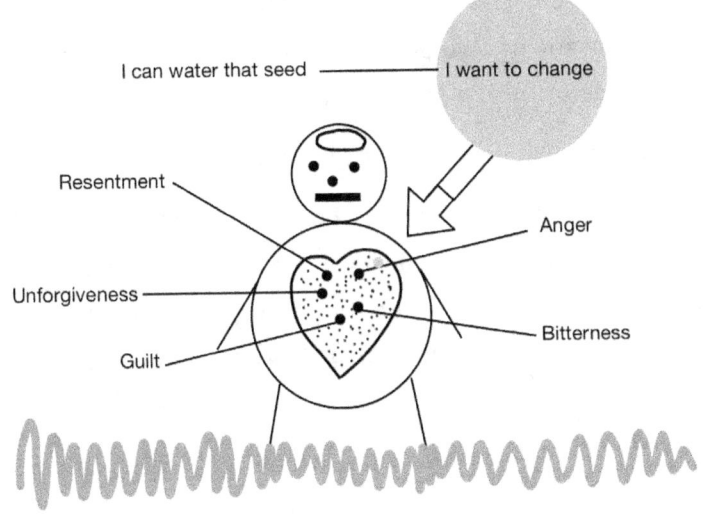

when they are clearly not ready, therefore shipwrecking their rehabilitation. I see many of those families later on and they are not together anymore. This is because when they took the person back they were okay for the short term but it wasn't long before they were a full-blown druggie again.

However, this time the damage that was done is unrepairable, a bit like the married couple in this story. When a person goes into rehab it's not always easy, like life you have good days and bad days, but they are all needed to help us to grow. On the bad days the fella rings his partner looking for cracks to see if they would take him back if he left and if he sees one, it doesn't take much, then he is off. It is so sad. I'm not saying that rehabilitation is the answer for everyone either.

- Is the seed in his or her heart that says they want to change?

The desire to want to change must be greater than the desire to want to stay the same. The desire to want to change must be greater than the desire to use drugs. They must be at the point where they want to change because they want to change, not because someone else is telling them to.

- Are they doing it for the right reasons?

Are they doing it for them, for their Mum and Dad, are they doing it for their wife or just to get their children back? If they are then they are doing it for the wrong reasons. They must want to do it because they want to and not because someone else is telling them to.

- Are they at a point they will do whatever it takes to change their life?

When I take a fella in I want to know for sure that they are serious about turning their life around, so I have a great deal of non-negotiable rules. No smoking, no mobile phone, no TV except PG and family rated movies, work from Monday to Friday without pay for the first part of the duration of the programme, just to name a few. More often than not when I take them in, I take them there and then on the spot. If they're not prepared to come in right then and there then they are not serious, as far as I'm concerned.

- Are they willing to go cold turkey to detox?

Most drug addicts have an addictive nature so I don't believe it's okay to take them off one drug; just to stick them on another, I don't think it's right. A great deal of addicts swap an illegal addiction for a legal one. They go from the meth to Valium or from the heroin to Methadone. Well, not with me they're not! Its cold turkey or they go somewhere else. What I do works, why on earth would you give a person more drugs when they have an addictive nature, it's not on.

Sure, they are sick for a week or so and sure, many of them find it's days before they get a full night's sleep. But hey, if you want to stick battery acid and other chemicals in your veins and your system, there will be a consequence. Some of those consequences are when you stop using drugs you're going to get very little sleep and also you're going to get sick for a while. So in short, cold turkey works otherwise their brains look for the chemical to do what it is you're trying to teach them to do.

- Are they at a point where there is no other option other than the one to change their life?

If they have any excuses in any way, shape or form, then it's not good enough. They must, and I mean must, be prepared to do whatever it takes especially if they are coming to me.

The next day comes and he can't get out of bed. He sleeps one day then two and then three and it moves into four, the only time he is out of bed is to go to the toilet or have a quick snack.

"Many families have no idea about drugs. They don't realise that a person can stay up for 16 days plus with no sleep."

Like I've said previously, "They should not have taken him in the home," but they did. What normally happens here is that he will sleep for a few days, resting his body and giving it a break from the weeks and months of abuse he has put it through. Most families only know five percent of what he has been up to. A lot of what he has been up to they would not think possible, as many have no idea about drugs. They don't realise that a person can stay up for 16 days plus with no sleep. While he is sleeping the family spend a great deal of time searching the yellow pages or the internet, trying to find a place that will take him, only to be told time and time again things like:

- We are full.
- We have a three-month waiting list.
- He will need to be the one to make an appointment.
- Unless the person wanting the help is the one that makes the call, we can't help.
- The person's age is between 13 & 33.
- He must be over the age of 18.
- He must go to a detox centre before he comes here.
- He must be three weeks clean before we will take him (believe it or not, one of the rehabs I know have that condition of entry).

When you start hearing all this in the back of your mind you start to think well maybe this is not going to be as easy as I thought it would be after all, and yes, that's right, it's not.

My hope for you, in reading this book, is that you might be right where I am talking about in certain parts of this book and you would be encouraged to act now. You may not yet be at that point but after having read this whole book and seeing your story unfolding just as I have written it, the reality of what you're about to go through, will prompt you to act sooner rather than later by setting the boundaries you need to set. My hope for you is that this would be the case for you so that it will spare you and your family some unnecessary grief and long-term pain.

I'm trying to think what I would tell you to do now that you have let him in the home and I don't know what to say, other than you have made a mistake and that it's a stupid one that you may live to regret. However there is hope but are you and your family willing to do what it takes to embrace it? It's going to take teamwork and a big sacrifice on everyone's behalf.

If you are going to bring him into the home, you must consider what you will have to go through if you are going to take this option and before you do.

- The thing you need to consider is that this may be realistically for up to six to eight weeks: are you prepared for that?

- You need to be prepared not to let him leave your sight in any way, shape or form until he has gone into a rehabilitation facility, who is going to watch him, how much commitment are you prepared to make?

- You must be prepared to drive him to all appointments, yes, all of them as he can't be trusted.

- You must not let him or her have a mobile phone or social media such as Facebook. It's important that he doesn't connect with old mates.

- You must be prepared not to let him have contact with any of his past associates, as well as be willing to do what it takes to enforce it. It's going to be hard work, are you sure?

- You must be willing to confront him or her on the smallest thing, taking a "one strike and you're out" policy. Zero tolerance, seriously.

- You must draw up a memorandum of understanding document for them to sign before they move into your home. This is a MUST for you, your families and all involved.

- In that document, you MUST put down everything you want them to agree to before moving in to your home and every few days revisit it with them, reminding them of their obligations. Put in place review periods where you can renegotiate what you have put down.

- If you are going to bring him or her in the home, you must sit with them prior and make sure that they know what they are agreeing to.

- Get yourself some support from family members. Maybe they might like to share the load with you until you can get them into a rehabilitation centre, as a group of people united will be more likely to get it across the line.

- Identify what your main goal is: "A changed life". Now break it down into five or ten short-term goals to get there with an assessment at each step of the way.

Memorandum of Understanding

You must put together a memorandum of understanding and also be prepared to set a whole heap of boundaries like what I have listed above such as:

- They need to understand that this is only a SHORT-TERM agreement until they can get themselves into a rehab.

- They need to understand that they must be prepared to ring the same rehab every day themselves, showing the rehabs that they are serious about wanting to change.

- They must agree that they will go to a rehab regardless if it's smoking or non-smoking, regardless of what the rules are that they will go in, at the first opportunity.

- They must agree there is to be no using of drugs on or off the property while they are staying with you.

- Agree also that they will not bring drugs on the property or bring people who use them to the property.

- They must agree to attend some form of counselling until they can get themselves into rehab.

- Also agree to undertake or be subjected to random urine testing where and when required.

- They must pay towards rent and food as well as bills to do with their lodging where possible, make sure you charge them even though they get little from Centrelink as you must appear to always be strict and without room for movement in your agreement.

- Make sure that they do their share of the chores around the home such as wash, cook and clean.

- Not bring anyone to the property without permission, in any way.

- They should agree that there must be some level of transparency as trust is something to be earned, not expected.

- Establish a review time where together you can review the agreement that was put in place before he or she came to stay, at least on a weekly basis.

- The two parties should also put in place an exit strategy in case it doesn't work. Something where if one party feels that it's not going to work out, then they have the others permission to back out without either party taking offence.

- They must absolutely agree not to use the phone or have a phone or use any media such as Facebook. This one is very important as they will do whatever they can to deceive you.

- They must also agree if he does not do his part that he will agree to leave the property immediately, no questions asked.

Now when you look at the list above you have put most if not all of it down. It's important to give them some say or input into the agreement as it helps them feel that they are allowed to have a say, even though at the start you may not take on board any of what they say, but over time you may.

"Don't feel bad that you're asking too much from them because you're not."

Remember you have a lot of short-term goals to get to the main one. This is going to take some time and will not happen overnight. Don't feel bad that you're asking too much from them because you're not. You need to put as many boundaries in place as possible, until you have a peace in your heart.

Finally on day four he is moving around the house so they try to approach him about a couple of rehabs, half-heartedly he shows a little effort and attends one of the appointments but because they don't allow smoking it's not the one for him, so they try a few more. The next one is too far away and the one after that has too many lead up appointments and it seems too hard but he agrees just to keep the family happy.

He sleeps another night and when he wakes up in the morning he says that he just has to duck up the road to pick up his phone, "I won't be a sec" he says, then four hours later he gets back. You can tell he has been up to no good by the way he has all his energy back and by the way he is talking. You confront him and he does what he always does.

He turns it on you saying, "You don't trust me, no matter how hard I try you always have a go at me! Why should I try if you always do that to me?"

In the end you have a big argument and he says "stuff you" and leaves. He blames you for why he is leaving and makes you feel like you stuffed it up even though he was the one that ducked off and got himself some drugs but you doubt now if you were right, even though you knew you were. So now he and his brother are not talking and the cycle continues again. He has just had a week's break off the gear thanks to his brother and he goes straight like a dog to the vomit and a pig to the mud.

You can start to tell the warning signs that a person is not committed to change when you have to do all the work in making the appointments and when you do line up an appointment, he only goes to keep you happy. You can sense it by his body language and lack of enthusiasm. What he will try to do is see if you will budge on your stance on him having to go to rehab.

After a few days' rest, he will want drugs as his mind will automatically go there. He will wake up and the first thing on his mind will be where can I get on, who can I call to get some? He will come to you and make every excuse under the sun to be able to duck up the road for a sec, or he will make a few phone calls seeing if he can get it dropped off.

For the drug addict, especially those on the heavier drugs, if they don't do it you should be shocked because they need the drug to feel normal. Because you had no idea what he was up to you let him go out and when he comes back you can tell he has been up to no good. All of a sudden he is a willing participant again, wanting to change and making your job a little easier. When you confront him I would be surprised if he didn't argue with you in return. He will deny it black and blue, but you know. You can tell in your heart you've been had but he turns it on you, you have been here before.

This again is typical of what happens in families that one by one each of the family have tried to help him but in the end they all feel used, abused, taken advantage of and disrespected. By now they have been lied to, stolen from and much more. They don't know where else to turn. They honestly thought he was ready and the moment they had waited for is now gone. He has slipped back to being a D because he is rested up and ready for another round.

All the family are angry at each other, one says we should have done it this way and another says we should have done it that way. More division, bitterness, anger and the cycle continues. He hits the drugs for another four months or so until one day he rings his sister up asking and begging for money.

Apparently he owes the bikies $2000 and if he doesn't pay it within 24 hours it doubles to $4000 and another $2000 every other day.

She panics and gives him the $2000 even though she knows she shouldn't. She didn't tell her husband or anyone else because she knew what they would say. Deep in her heart she knows that she will never see the cash again. Eight weeks later it happens again. He rocks up at her doorstep, bloodied and bruised, crying saying they are going to kill him. The bikies have given him 24 hours to come up with $10,000 or they have threatened to kill him and attack his family if he doesn't pay. She is in panic mode and doesn't know what to do so she rings Dad and he rings his other son and they start arguing again about what they should do or who should do what. In the end the sister is so scared for her brother that she pays the cash because he promised her if she did, he would go to rehab or do whatever it is that she asked from him. She pays the cash then he disappears, because she paid the bills that took months to accumulate. Now he has no debt and he goes back like a dog to its vomit and a pig to the mud and the cycle continues.

Normally many families will face this many, many times over the addict's life, until they get to the point where they get burnt once too many times. One by one they all write him off, vowing never to help him again. Many families get burnt financially on more than one occasion.

Many just continue to get burnt because they say to themselves, "I don't want to see my loved one die," and so they continue to pay the bills, slowly killing their children in the process, you might think that's harsh but it's true.

The last thing you should do is pay any bills, especially drug debts, as in many cases they learn from their mistakes and just become smarter addicts. When dealing with an addict you can expect to be let down, lied to, stolen from, deceived, cheated and manipulated, just to name a few things.

> ***"Many families don't want to see their loved one die, so they continue to pay the bills, slowly killing their children in the process."***

There are many drug dealers out there and it's not just the bikies who will threaten the person with the double up job. If you owe $2000 they say for every day you are late you owe another $2000 taking the total to $4000 and rising. This is normal so don't be shocked when you hear it. Whatever you do, DO NOT pay it. Give him nothing as all you are doing is putting drugs in his veins. There are many other groups who threaten to break his legs or worse, but it sounds a lot worse than it is for a person who has never experienced this before.

At worst, he may get a good kick in the head or a broken kneecap but that may teach him a lesson or two and personally I don't think that's a bad thing as it comes with the territory.

You need to leave as many hooks in his back as possible. Remember we want him as an E; we want him to come to the point where he will want to change his life. I deal with many fellas who come into Shalom with debts to various clubs and I help the fellas and their families navigate through what it takes to clear the debt. You paying the bill doesn't help them in the way you need to, at all. Every decision they make has a consequence. If you continue to spare them from the consequences of their choices, they will never learn.

I have sat with the mother who has lost her son due to an overdose and with the Dad whose child has committed suicide. I have sat with the families at the gravesite who have had to lower their child into the grave, jumping in after the coffin is lowered into the hole. I've sat with wives who have lost husbands and children, their Dads. I understand the risk of drug use and understand the pain, both mentally and physically.

I understand what will be going through their minds as they have read what I have written, and as they think about putting into practice what I have suggested. I will stand by what I have written and what I say. I would like to be straight up with you when I say there is a good chance your child or loved one may die, but they are slowly killing themselves anyway. If you don't do something soon there is also a good chance they may end up in and out of a mental ward for the rest of their lives or killing someone else, as all this unfolds. You have a choice to make. You have some choices to make.

TOUGH LOVE

CHAPTER ~7~

Ten Questions From The Other Side

What I have done is written ten questions that I have asked family members who have gone through the battle to see a loved one come out the other side free from addiction. I have asked them questions that I hope will help you not make the same mistakes that they have made.

1. How has your family changed through the journey of addiction?
2. With the chance to do it again, what would you do differently and why?
3. What did you do that you shouldn't have?
4. What did you try that worked?

5. What did not work?
6. What changes did you see taking place?
7. What suggestions do you have for families?
8. How did you enable?
9. How did you look after yourself and other family members?
10. Where did you go for help and what was the outcome?

Joy B's story

Paul was my firstborn, a much wanted and loved son after three daughters from my husband's previous marriage. He was still only five and an elder brother to three younger siblings. School years were happy. My husband never wanted for work and all the children did well at school. We had lots of holidays and the children participated in various extracurricular activities. Paul especially loved his sport and drama. He was a high achiever at secondary school, a private Catholic college. He went on to UWA to study a BA.

It is around this time that I recall that problems started. Paul went from a homebody to being out all the time and I went from knowing all his mates to being unaware of his social crowd and activities. This did not ring any particular alarm bells at the time as I considered it par for the course for an 18-year-old university student.

After initial good marks in the first year Paul began to fail and pull out of classes and lie about the reasons for this. He still lived at home but we never saw any of his friends and he gravitated to a new life which his family had no part.

We became aware of marijuana use and had a number of conversations around this issue which inevitably led to shouting and arguments. On one occasion Paul stated he enjoyed what he was doing, believed it was harmless and that he'd be continuing whether we liked it or not. He was told then that if that was the decision he had made he could no longer live at home with his three younger siblings, then teenagers aged 13, 14 and 16.

Paul did leave at that point but came and went over the following year. In late 1999 while living at home Paul developed meningococcal septicaemia and very quickly became critically ill. Fortunately he was hospitalised in time and treated successfully. I was hopeful this life/death situation would be a wake-up call but it was not. In 2000 we paid for Paul to go to Italy to live in a religious community of young people from all around the world who give witness to "Love one another as I have loved you." This also was of no lasting benefit. Paul was overseas 18 months and never lived at home again. On his return to Perth, his life took on a chaotic trend as things spiralled out of control. It is called a downward spiral because there is no way to stop it and it just gets worse and worse until the inevitable crash.

Paul re-commenced university but then stopped attending again. He had a series of accommodations with dubious housemates. He sometimes worked, sometimes went to counselling, sometimes communicated. The following 13 years were a rollercoaster, with Paul fluctuating between employment and being in communication to homelessness and non-communication (sometimes weeks, sometimes years).

Friends would tell me, "It's a phase he's going through," or "He's young. Give him time," or "Look at your other three. Paul will turn out okay too."

I desperately wanted to believe my well-intentioned friends, while deep down inside knowing that this was not how it was.

Emotionally, I was in turmoil and felt completely overwhelmed. I felt worried that all my emotional energy was being spent on Paul and this may lead to resentment from his brothers and sister. I felt helpless as every avenue I tried yielded no benefit. I felt isolated from my friends. The ones who knew of Paul's circumstances would never speak of him for fear of upsetting me. The ones who knew nothing could only wonder why I only ever mentioned three of my children. The son I did know had become a stranger.

"The counsellor asked us to name all the things we had done to try and help our son over the years. In 10 minutes, a huge whiteboard was full with everything from giving him money and food and advice to arranging job interviews and driving him to countless therapy sessions. 'And what lasting benefit has any of this brought?' we were asked."

I was deeply afraid of losing Paul not only as a member of our family but I was also scared for his physical wellbeing. He may die due to the lifestyle he lived. Perhaps he would even take his own life. Sometimes I felt like Paul was already dead. I did not see him, talk with him or know any information about him or his whereabouts. He did not exist in my life except for my thoughts, memories and prayers. At times I was close to despair and even envied a friend whose son, Paul's age, had died of cancer. She received sympathy and kind words and could slowly begin to move through the grieving process. I was living with my agony every day with no end in sight. How could I ever have believed my pain and grief was equal to hers? This was indicative of how emotionally low I had fallen.

In desperation my husband and I sought out a counsellor for ourselves. She asked us to name all the things we had done to try and help our son over the years. In 10 minutes a huge whiteboard was full with everything from giving him money and food and advice to arranging job interviews and driving him to countless therapy sessions. "And what lasting benefit has any of this brought?" we were asked.

As I gazed at the multiple lengthy lists, I was dismayed to realise that the answer was "None."

This was a real wake-up call to me. From that day I made a conscious decision to stop intervening in Paul's life but simply to be there for him, supportive in word and prayer. This was a major shift in my thinking and my mental health stabilised and improved. I could only be there for Paul when he chose to be in touch and reassure him he was loved unconditionally as he broke his word over and over.

Sometimes he was in a good place, – employed, drug-free, fit and healthy and communicating with his family but it never lasted. Time after time our hopes were dashed and replaced by fear. Prayer was my only sustenance much of the time.

It was surely answered near midnight on New Year's Eve 2014 when Paul phoned and said, "Mum, can you come and pick me up?"

I collected him from the roadside near an abandoned building where he was living with his worldly possessions in a small backpack. Within three days, Paul chose life over death when he entered Shalom House. There is no resemblance in appearance nor attitude to the wreck that came home that night.

1. How has your family changed through the journey of addiction?

As our door was always open to Paul, should he choose to make changes, I hoped the other children would see that no matter how serious a problem they may ever have, that we would be a support and they would never be turned away. At times the children did say they felt they were disciplined harshly for minor indiscretions. They considered Paul's behaviour so much worse yet he was always helped and not punished. It did affect how I related to and disciplined Paul's brothers and sister. Of course they were not as close to him as they were to one another as they were not involved in his life nor him in theirs. I was very stressed, worried, anxious and depressed to the point of it affecting my health and being on medication. This impacted the family greatly. For example, I could not attend my other son's 21st birthday celebration. Now my perspective has changed in that I feel I am more compassionate and non-judgemental.

2. With the chance to do it again, what would you do differently and why?

I would have confronted the problem earlier and taken it more seriously. We were incredibly naïve and I should have been better informed – forewarned is forearmed. I believed excuses too readily due to my unworldly lack of judgement but also because I wanted to as the alternative was too horrible to entertain.

3. What did you do that you shouldn't have?

We spent countless hours questioning, arguing and pleading with Paul and forever making excuses for his behaviour. We would say he was unwell, lost, still sorting himself out instead of saying he was a drug addict.

4. What did you try that worked?

We always kept the channels of communication open from our side. He knew we found his lifestyle choices totally unacceptable but we were always here and ready to help when he decided to change.

5. What did not work?

Many things worked for short periods but nothing for the long term. Many hours of counselling, nearly dying, going overseas to get away from bad influences all had no lasting benefit.

6. What changes did you see taking place?

Physical changes with poor health, weight loss, bad skin. Changes in personality and behaviour – lying and stealing and broken promises about everything.

7. What suggestions do you have for families?

Have a united front within your family. Parents need to be on the same page and follow through with rules and conditions that they make. This is not only for the good of your child, but also to protect your own mental and physical health.

Yield control in trying to sort out the details of your child's life. Accept that it is their wrong choice and they must face the consequences.

Do not say, "If I do not give him a bed, he will be homeless." Do not say, "I must pay his debts or he will go to jail."

By his actions he has chosen homelessness and prison. Hardest lesson of all is, "He may die if I don't help him."

Daily he is choosing to die by taking drugs.

Enabling your child to continue in his destructive life is totally unproductive and probably will prolong the period before an individual decides to seek help.

8. How did you enable?

I enabled in almost every way possible except for having Paul live at home. I enabled him to get and keep jobs by making excuses to employers ("He's sick.") I found accommodation and furnished it, I bought food, gave money, drove him to appointments, made job interviews and paid for counselling.

9. How did you look after yourself and other family members?

My husband and I tried to focus on what was happy in the lives of the other children and often "out of sight, out of mind," was my method of coping as sometimes Paul was absent for years and we had no idea where or how he was.

10. Where did you go for help and what was the outcome?

Early on I sought advice from the Alcohol and Drug phone support line. This was of zero benefit as I was told it was a phase and I was worrying unnecessarily. I believed them because I considered they knew more than me and also because I wanted to.

We really closed ranks as a family and did not seek much outside information or help. My husband and I on one occasion went to counselling and this was extremely beneficial and saved my sanity.

It gave me the courage to step back and not shoulder all the guilt and responsibility for Paul's choices. She pointed out that we had been enabling him for years to no avail and it was time to stop.

The outcome was that from that day I took a step back from the practical involvement in Paul's life and suddenly the burden was somewhat lifted.

Finally after 16 years Paul made the choice to enter Shalom House and the outcome has been nothing short of a miracle. The love and true charity of the team there has been a wonderful revelation and our gratefulness to them knows no bounds. These good Samaritans take in strangers, broken men and transform them in body and spirit.

Gail C's story

When you are blessed with the news you are carrying precious cargo, "a baby," nothing can take away the elated feeling you have, at no point do you ever imagine the extreme rollercoaster ride you are about to encounter as a mother.

My eldest child as a baby did most things by the book although usual milestones came quicker than most, he crawled at 4 months and was walking by the time he was 8 months old, as he grew up and found his voice, we realised very soon he was going to be quite a handful and mostly did the complete opposite of what he was asked. He struggled through school, so as a loving devoted mother I did my best and then some to protect and stand up for him. We tried lots of different approaches with the help of some clinical psychologists and eventually trying him on ADHD medication, this worked for a very short period of time.

Even though all these struggles were going on our son had and has a heart of gold, he was always very polite and courteous when he was at anyone's house. And most of the time very helpful when he wanted to be.

It started in early teen years when he would steal my cigarettes and sell his ADHD medication to pay for marijuana for himself, my fears started escalating when I realised if we tried to discipline him or lay down ground rules he would very quickly lash out, mainly at me. As time went by, he spent little time at home and more and more time with families that allowed pot smoking and the like. This cut really deep, because I thought we had taught our kids right from wrong and that would be enough, but it's not because they make their own choices and have the influences of a big wide world.

Through the years we tried many avenues of help from counsellors to psychiatrists to drug rehab including Holyoake and a place in the city somewhere where he stayed for about 3 weeks. When he came out he was clean for all of three days, as when we cleaned out his room of drugs or paraphernalia we didn't realise that he had hidden drugs in the lining of a motorbike helmet.

> **"If I locked our son out of our home, he would break in while we were at work, taking tiles off the roof and coming in through the manhole."**

At times, there would be suspicious activity around our house, things went missing and stuff was damaged. Our attention at one point was drawn to a large number of huge bags of marijuana on his bed (which we saw on a photo on Facebook). If I locked him out of our home, he would break in while we were at work, taking tiles off the roof and coming in through the manhole. I didn't trust him to be in our home if no-one was there to supervise. I was very quickly running out of any trust or respect for my son, I felt sick with sorrow and fear of what was happening. People had turned up to retrieve drugs he had ripped off and to ask us for money he owed; we never paid them or gave into their threats.

I had suspicions for a while that he was doing much more than just pot smoking. It was 2013 I think when I searched my son's room and found a glass bulb type thing, which I knew was used for smoking 'crack'.

When I confronted him he broke down in tears and said "No, you're not supposed to know," and he said he would get help to stop, this was one of the many times he said he would stop and get help. He didn't.

> ***"I'm watching my son die, he's killing himself slowly and destroying his family at the same time and worse than that, he doesn't care."***

I believed his lies a few times because I wanted nothing more than my baby boy back, this beautiful miracle we had brought into the world now hated us. He must hate us — why else would he lie, steal, smash up the house, have his younger brother and sister fear him, allow "strangers" into our home?

Why would anyone want to sit back and watch our world crumble, watch your mother cry with absolute despair and grief? Yes, grief, that's what it is.

"I'm watching my son die, he's killing himself slowly and destroying his family at the same time and worse than that, he doesn't care."

Okay, that's it. We have to put our foot down, so we told him he had to leave the house. So he would for a while then he would come back broken and scared. He would say he's not going to do drugs anymore and typically we would believe him, take him back, then bang all over again, it doesn't take long for them to slip back into the same world of lies deceit and drugs, because we are suckers for our kids and he pulled at our heart strings all the time.

As he had tried suicide himself a few times I guess I thought if we kicked him out for good then something bad would happen and it would be my fault. Have you ever felt pain on the inside, unbelievable pain that feels literally like your heart has been put into a vice and is being squeezed of all it has? That's what it feels like when you find your child hanging in their bedroom.

We had gotten into many heated arguments. One day while he was home I had asked him to leave the house before I went to work (he refused) and this ended badly with the house smashed up. I had bruises on my legs and a black eye, my youngest child was cowering in the corner of a room sobbing. He got so angry he was right up in my face so while I was on the phone to the police, I hit my son in the face with the phone and split his eye open. He took off and the police issued a warrant for his arrest and a VRO.

This was an extremely low point for me at which I slipped into depression. I cried all the time and took anti-depressants for a while to keep me functioning to a degree. We decided we couldn't stay in our home any more so we sold it to make a fresh start, our son was gone and had no idea we had done this.

We went to one of the houses he was staying in, "It should have been condemned." We spent all day one day cleaning it, I have never been in such an emotional state, cleaning up drug paraphernalia that my son was using; once, he knocked a bowl out of my hand that had ice in it because he was afraid I would get it on me.

We thought we were helping; we would stock up the fridge and pantry for him week after week. This made us feel better as we felt at least he's eating healthy food. This was clearly enabling him to use whatever money he got to purchase drugs, along with whatever else he did to get the money for drugs, stealing, grand theft auto and I believe some other really bad stuff.

He had gone from a fit, healthy kid to a skinny, gaunt shadow of a person. It broke my heart to see him like this. The lies and deceit continued. At one point he had cellulitis in his ankle from picking at bugs under his skin "that weren't there" and he almost lost his foot.

"Years prior, I had taken out funeral insurance and kept it going because I truly believed that at one point we would be burying our son sooner or later."

So a year or so passed by and we moved into our brand new house, to make a fresh start. Once again we let our son come back. He was back and forth for a year and a bit until the last straw, our daughter found needles in his room.

"Okay that's it, I'm done," is the thought that went through my mind. It took a fair bit of talking, planning and convincing each other that the best thing to do would be to kick him out. We had done this so many times before and he begs to come home because he is starving and has nowhere to go.

I've neglected to say and this may sound terrible, but years prior I had taken out funeral insurance and kept it going because I truly believed that at one point we would be burying our son sooner or later. The reality of this ice addiction and alike, "People die," also my brothers had taken drugs with our son before. I know I should forgive them, but I still can't. One of my brothers I have not had contact with in years, because of his dealings with my boy, they weren't/aren't exactly positive role models; however he has made his own choices with consequence.

I recall going to prison to visit our son. We went through the process of booking in to see him. You have to hand in everything you carry, you can take nothing in through security. We stood in line with every other visitor, and while I stood there as the drug dog went up and down the line of people. The dog sat right in front of me not once but three times, so then I was taken into a room, asked if I had drugs as that is what the dog had picked up on me.....me! Really, I am the most anti-drug person standing in that line. So then we were informed that it would be a non-contact visit, and had to watch him through bulletproof glass as he was clearly coming down off whatever he had been taking for God knows how long.

He was very angry with us at this point and he couldn't understand why we didn't bail him out at that time, (he understands now) and on the way out I literally couldn't feel my legs. My husband held on tight as we walked back to our car, both of us absolutely devastated at not only having to visit our son in prison, but seeing him in such a terrible state, there were many times of feeling numb, helpless and so very sad.

I needed to be there to support our other two children and my husband. I had to go to work and do things normal people do, people without a drug addict for a son. This was really hard, my heart and head were torn. Nothing made sense, life just carried on and I just waited for the next thing to happen because the next thing always happened.

My life was full of "what ifs." You know when you are asked to retrace or recall all the things that happened and unfolded. Your mind goes on a tangent and things pop into your mind at random moments, so much happened in such a short time.

At times we were helping our son on his path to destruction and I truly believe he would have killed himself and knowing what we know now, we would have been part of this. That's when I realised it had to stop as I said earlier, "last straw" with his little sister finding needles in his room. So the talk went like this, keeping in mind I had called Peter Lyndon-James three years prior to ask if he could take our son. But our boy wasn't ready for that as he didn't think his drug addiction had taken control.

We approached an already angry son with little to no emotion: "We had nothing left."

"Son, here's the thing, you cannot stay in our house anymore, not as a drug addict. You have an option, you pack your bags to go live on the streets and continue on this path or you take this number and ask Peter for help."

We copped a lot of abuse and he tried the emotional blackmail, you know the kind, "You don't care about me, you don't know what it's like," and all the explicit language that comes with it. This time it didn't work. We were done and he was at the bottom. He had nothing left, nowhere to go.

He made a decision that night to change his life for the better. He entered the Shalom House programme the next day. What a relief, I hadn't cried that much in a long time. Absolute tears of joy and for the first time in a very long time we actually slept peacefully knowing exactly where he was. I am still on guard I think I will be for a really long time.

1. How has your family changed through the journey of addiction?

Our immediate family consists of our three children ages 21, 17 and 14, my husband and myself. It's safe to say we have been to hell and back, constantly on tender hooks wondering what was going to happen next. Our younger two children learnt at quite a young age to dislike their brother and his addiction. We all put barriers up and didn't have much to look forward to, however in some way, addiction has taught our two younger children to despise drugs and everything they do and change about a person. All of us lost trust in everything, I particularly became very suspicious of everyone, especially people Brodie had contact with. We all became angry, emotionally drained and very unhappy.

2. With the chance to do it again, what would you do differently and why?

I would really hope I didn't have the chance to do it again. Methamphetamine is an evil drug and the people who make it and distribute it destroy lives (lots of them). We have the strength to say, "No, you're not doing this to us again, we love you, but you cannot stay in our home," and ask him to leave and if he didn't, an instant restraining order would be sought.

3. What did you do that you shouldn't have?

We constantly rescued him from situations, we would get phone calls in the middle of the night, that he would very quickly forget about. He constantly asked for food and cigarettes of which we would go and buy for him (silly idea) even though we didn't hand him cash money, we funded him by paying for his food and cigarettes.

4. What did you try that worked?

We had tried counselling services through Mental Health, anti-psychosis medication which seemed to work for a very short period of time, I guess because it was just a band-aid covering up the real issue.

5. What did not work?

Nothing seemed to work to be honest. Everything we tried seemed to only work to a small degree, and I think in part that is because he would just go through the motions of what we wanted him to do, (he really didn't want to stop his drug use) and in part because we rescued him from time to time I guess we prolonged the situation. Kicking him out of home didn't work until he had burned his bridges with everyone, unfortunately he always seemed to land himself a bed with like people (drug addicts).

6. What changes did you see taking place?

Brodie went from a good-looking, fit guy to a terrible skeleton of himself, he had sores on his body, he actually nearly lost his leg at one stage to cellulitis. He lied about absolutely everything, he became increasingly more aggressive physically and verbally, he would go through stages of psychosis and severe paranoia, he stole from people and had no remorse about that at the time. It's as if he thought the world owed him a favour.

7. What suggestions do you have for families?

I would strongly suggest you protect yourself and other family members right from the onset, don't pay for stuff for them, absolutely never give them any cash of any sort, don't pay off their drug debts, set very strict rules for your home and family and stick to them, don't deviate. Don't get angry, it really doesn't help. Let them know you love them always but are not willing to let them destroy you or people close to you.

They make their own choices and as much as we as parents try to take as much control of that as possible (natural instinct I think) they are their own person and while in the state they put themselves in are their own worst enemy.

8. How did you enable?

Went and picked him up out of the gutter, gave him a nice warm bed to sleep off whatever he was on (then after a few days he would be straight back on it). I also bought a weekly shop for him and bought him cigarettes, clothes, bedding (this is while he wasn't living at home) in our minds at least he was eating, but in doing so allowed him to spend whatever money he got on drugs.

9. How did you look after yourself and other family members?

At times, we didn't really look after ourselves, we just lived, got up, went to work, came home, cooked dinner, all the while wondering what he's doing; if someone knocked on the front door, we would all think the worst. The times we did relax a bit and feel somewhat "normal", we would get a phone call from Brodie asking us to go and get him, so it began again.

It's only in the last 10 months or so we have learned to be happy and truly enjoy what we have and relax, life doesn't have to be a struggle. We have the strength, ability and knowledge to put plans in place to protect ourselves against this happening again.

10. Where did you go for help and what was the outcome?

A. We have been to Mental Health — outcome being they have very limited resources and don't have the time to spend on drug addicts. Generally they are handed more drugs to try get them to stop the drugs (this does not work).

B. Brodie went to DAYS (drug and alcohol youth services) for a couple of weeks (that's how long the programme is) then you have to go on a 3-month waiting list for the next step, as soon as he got out of DAYS he was straight back into the drugs.

C. He attended Holyoake's for counselling, he would come out of his appointments and tell me his counsellor reckons he doesn't have a problem. I think he was trying to convince himself and me that he didn't have a problem.

D. Finally when he hit the absolute bottom and we had absolutely had enough and were completely done, he contacted Peter Lyndon-James at Shalom and entered the programme. This is much better approach to getting these men clean, as their lives are brought back to basics and rebuilt without drugs. They are re-programmed, if you like, to make good choices in their lives so they can go out into society and live like normal people and not be a blight on society and although he didn't totally complete the programme, he has come a really long way; however, he knows our zero tolerance to drug use, and we will not hesitate to ask him to leave our happy place if he pushes those boundaries and buttons.

Brodie's Story [Gail's son]

Howzit going, my name is Brodie. I'm twenty years old and currently a resident at Shalom House, located in the Swan Valley. I have been in the programme now for approximately 3 months. I've been making bad decisions for about the last 7 years. I came from a good home and have a good upbringing. I have a younger brother and sister, and my family mean the world to me. Growing up, I was pretty normal, raised in Bullsbrook until around Grade 6.

Dad got a job in Broome driving trucks and so we shifted up there. I was never the cleverest kid in school and didn't think I was real smart either. I used to play up a fair bit but compensated by being a smart aleck in the playground. I felt I'd fit in by being one of the cool kids, and got a fair bit of attention for all the wrong reasons. This continued into high school where the cool kids turned into the stoner kids. I started smoking pot, stealing my mum's durries and drinking alcohol. It wasn't long until she clicked on.

Dad got a job back in Perth and so we moved to Ellenbrook. Entering a new school half way through Year 8, I once again became the new kid on the block. It was a learning curve getting used to the change from being a country kid from Broome, to living in the outer suburbs of Perth. As I made friends, I ended up choosing the wrong ones. I began to drink and smoke pot again. I realised that I could sell my ADD medication for a profit and the money I made, I used to buy more pot and to start selling it. By the time I was 16, I had met my childhood sweetheart and we had my beautiful son, Krystian. She left me two months before he was born and that's when the wheels started to fall off. My mates introduced me to meth and I found myself doing heaps of crime, thinking I was invincible. Violent assaults and grand theft auto landed me in prison for a short time. Knowing some of the fellas inside made it easier than I had expected. I wanted to change my life but I didn't know how to do it.

The pain from not being able to see my son caused a lot of depression and increased my anxiety. My drug use got worse until it ruined my relationship with my parents and my siblings. All the bad things in life made me try to commit suicide. One day my dad found me hanging in my room and saved my life. I ended up losing everything and everyone I had ever cared about. I was living on the street with no money for food or anything. I called my mom and asked for her help and she picked me up and took me home. I took advantage of her kindness and that was the last straw.

She told me that I needed to change and if I didn't, they would move away to a place I would never know. I rang Peter and the next day I went into a meeting. He took me in as I was, and led me to the Lord. That very day I began to turn my life around. Since being in Shalom, I have developed a relationship with Jesus, that has helped me work through my anger, resentment and unforgiveness issues. My tolerance levels of others and level of genuine joy has increased more than I could ever imagine. I have restored my family relationships, and am making progress to see my son for the first time in over 3 years!

I've found that humbling myself and submitting control over to Peter has been the hardest thing I have had to do. But I know that anything worth something doesn't come easy. I'm on my way to becoming an apprentice Boiler Maker Welder and am positive about the direction that my life is headed.

I thank God every day for my brothers at Shalom, who are helping me along my journey to become a better man. I'm thankful for my family and all the support they have given me. Most of all, I thank the Lord for Peter Lyndon-James for helping me to turn my life around.

Brodie C

Diane's story

I am 52, married with 3 children. My husband is 17 years older than me and I am his third wife. We've been happily together for 34 years and married for 22. We have two sons and a daughter ranging from 26 down to 21. My husband has a son and daughter from his previous marriages. His son passed away in 1990 due to a head-on car crash.

This event changed my husband in the way he wanted to raise his new family. He decided to retire early (55) so he could spend more time with his growing family so we travelled a lot and he spent a lot of the time sailing with them and teaching them about sailing, as well as being there for them whenever he could.

My husband and I were very involved in the upbringing of our children, providing many sporting opportunities as well as educational opportunities.

Right from an early age our middle child was different. He was diagnosed with ADHD at the age of five and shortly after the paediatrician advised we give him dexies. It was a constant struggle getting the doses right, changing from drug to drug and dose to dose to try and get a happy medium. We had him at counselling, anger management counselling, psychologists, we tried coloured glasses, special diets, the lot.

By the time he was 13 he had been to three different high schools before I even tried home schooling him for a while. At the end of Year 9 at yet another school, he was expelled a day before graduating. The school he was at had a special Year 9 graduation ceremony which he wasn't allowed to go to and neither were we. I spent 6 months making a special scrapbook (as did all mums in that year) with all his life achievements shown in photos, poems and special notes from friends, family and godparents which were to be presented to him at this graduation, but I was never able to present it to him. This was the first of many events where my son broke my heart.

We ended up getting him into a special TAFE course for Year 10 where he was able to do Year 10 in six months. This is where he befriended his first unsavoury friend. Around this time is when he started smoking weed at TAFE at his friend's house (the friend's mother would provide it) and anywhere else. I was naive then. I had no idea except that his clothes smelled of smoke (or so I thought) and asked him to try not to be in the same room where friends were smoking as it was bad for his asthma. It wasn't cigarette smoke at all.

He finished six months at TAFE and graduated and a month later started an apprenticeship as a French polisher/spray painter. The trouble continued with me often being called to his TAFE to have a meeting with his lecturer about his behaviour. It was relentless and so frustrating, as well as embarrassing. He finished his apprenticeship – just. He was still smoking weed with his friends which I only found out after the company he worked for was having drug testing done the following week. His boss had been a great mentor through his apprenticeship and was always trying to keep him on the straight and narrow too. He organised for my son to be away on the day of drug testing as he knew that my son wouldn't pass and would have lost his apprenticeship, which was only months from completion.

My son went from job to job and relationship to relationship. Lost his driver's licence a few times and would have tried every drug possible from the time he was around 16 or 17. This was later revealed to me by my son himself. He then became involved with some bikies. After a shutdown stint he came home with wads of money and took out a loan to buy a Harley Davidson. He was always trying to find ways to pay the loan through different jobs. It was around this time I think he started with ICE but we didn't know this at the time. He was coming and going all the time and his moods were worse than ever. He was impossible to live with. Bedroom doors were smashed, furniture was being thrown around, he was yelling and abusing both me and his father. He would have the scariest punch ups with his older brother and his sister would go running to friends' houses and not want to come home because she was so scared.

We thought it best he moved out of home and as we had an investment rental empty at the time. We got him to move there with another girl so they could share the rent. BIG MISTAKE. Now he had a free run to do what he liked, when he liked and it was terrible. He was becoming out of control now. He was picked up in MY car at 4am because all other cars that he owned were off the road for one reason or another. He was brilliant in pulling cars apart but wasn't too good at putting them together again. In my car he had lots of money including counterfeit notes, baggies of ice, knives and a replica pistol. The police took him back to his house, then ours and searched from top to bottom; OUR family home, only to find his rifles under his bed instead of in the gun cabinet. Many charges were laid.

He was bailed to appear at another date. In the meantime he decided to swap his 4WD with an XR6 turbo ute. He did the deal but little did he know this ute still had $22,000 owing on it and the guy had obviously stopped paying his repayments. Our son was driving around in an incredibly powerful machine and he thought he was invincible. He eventually ended up in a police chase. At one stage he was driving down the wrong side of the freeway doing 200kmh. The police helicopter was commissioned and after about an hour they got him with stingers but he still kept on driving for a bit, eventually crashing into a ditch. He still tried to run through paddocks, over and under barbed wire, before they eventually pounced.

This little episode, as well as the other arrest, put him in jail for 6 months. It was absolutely heartbreaking. The funny thing is though, we felt a sense of relief in a way as we knew where he was and that he was being looked after, although it was in jail. After all the stress over the past few years my husband and I decided on a holiday, so we spent 6 weeks in Europe and we were able to enjoy this holiday as we knew our son was safe.

The time came for his release. By this time we had to sell the investment property. The actions of our son and the damage that he caused to the house had cost us dearly. We sold the house and we're lucky to be able to pay off bills but were left with nothing at the end of it. So.....our son came back to live with us. He had changed considerably for the better and was given the opportunity of a job by one of his previous employers.

Life was looking good. About two months into his parole he went out with the boys for a buck's night. At the end of the night he was waiting for a taxi with his mates when someone jumped the queue and jumped in to the taxi. Our son saw red and tried to grab the guy out of the front seat when someone in the back seat reached over and stabbed my son's hand. The taxi took off with my son running after it not realising he had been injured. When he looked down he realised he was in trouble. His hand had been stabbed cutting right through tendons and nerves. Surgery followed and work was cancelled. He was working as a rope access technician (commercial abseiler) at the time.

There was no way he could hang from ropes with only one working hand. Occupational therapy followed and as a result of not working, bills were piling up, including the repayments for his Harley. So due to boredom, frustration and desperation, he started dealing again. He had no license but was still jumping on his Harley to "meet with friends".

On ANZAC Day 2015, after a heated argument with his father and after throwing iron chairs through the front door, he attacked his father from behind, bringing him down to the ground, kicking him in the back a few times. His father is 69 years old and knew he shouldn't fight back, so just let himself fall to the ground. The police were called and our son was ordered to move on. He did for a while, but came back to get his phone and wallet.

The police were called again and he was arrested once more. We had lost him once more and we were not letting him back again. For the next few months he couch surfed, apparently, and was in a very bad way. It was around this time that my brother introduced us to one of his friends who has a rehab in Esperance. I spoke at length with her and she gave lots of support and advice. One of these pieces of advice was to cut all ties with our son. She said often that he needed to hit rock bottom if he was to ever have a chance of seeking help. We took her advice as hard as it was. It went totally against all my maternal instincts. We also continued with the VRO (past the 72 hours that the police imposed on that ANZAC Day).

At one point we had some hope as he agreed to contact Peter at Shalom House. A friend of ours drove him up from Mandurah all the way to some café near Midland to be accepted by Peter but during the interview got cold feet and declined Peter's offer. Our son eventually got himself in more and more trouble and was eventually arrested once again.

All the things he had been doing for those 6 months after ANZAC Day had finally caught up with him again. He was able to get bail, but the only people who were able to bail him out were his parents. Yes, us. We decided to NOT bail him out, so he stayed in jail on remand till he was finally released after 8 weeks.

And this is where we went wrong. We dropped the VRO against our son, not that he knew this. The first thing he did when released from the court house was walk to our place. After discussions and promises by him we took him in again. He had a girlfriend before going on remand and she was still in the picture when he got out, even though she was sleeping off her last binge on ICE for the first few days after he got out. In his desperation to get her back he got her name tattooed on his chest, as he was so scared of losing her. She was a piece of work though. She led him to believe that she was pregnant when she wasn't. She was to look after his clothes while he was inside but ended up selling them at some stage, and led him to believe they were stolen. He wouldn't be told though.

After only a few weeks at home and after more lies, we kicked him out yet again. He went and stayed with her father and although he was behaving himself, he was now involved with a woman who was mentally disturbed and still using drugs herself. After a few months we started talking again and I eventually helped him get a unit. She moved in like a rat up a drain pipe. He was working but she wasn't and had no intention of working or getting Centrelink.

He lost his job again and she was really causing havoc in the apartment complex. Complaints were coming in and after his first property inspection, he was terminated. There were smashed doors, nail polish dribbled all over carpets after she wrote profanities on the walls when he didn't come home on time and chips all over the plaster walls.

We helped him pack all his things and moved everything back here while we looked for another place for him. When we found a place we moved all his stuff in and, as expected, she was in there like a rat up a drain pipe again.

Again she was causing a fuss. He was desperately trying to do well this time around. He was not using and was getting drug tested randomly by his parole officer, so was too scared to use, as the last thing he wanted was to go back inside. It all came to a head one night where she pushed his buttons just once too often.

As he was screaming at her to leave his house, she called the police and he was arrested once more. After hours of questioning he was released and ordered HER to leave his house. She did for a bit but turned around and came back. He called the police again and they ended up arresting her this time and she was sent on her way.

Since this time my son has been trying to get his life back on track but there is no end to this girl's persistence. She has called the bikies on to him and he has been roughed up a few times now. Money has been extorted from him. He sold his last possession, an RX7 to pay them off. He knows that we will not be paying any of his past drug debts.

So this brings us to today……. He has started to hang around with "friends" from his past. He has stopped contacting me. He has lost yet another job. He has lost a lot of weight in a short time. My biggest fears have been realised. I feel we are back to square one again.

Fast forward 6 months………

He called me one day, asking if he could stay at our place. He was scared to stay at his home, as he felt that if he did, he would take his life. (I found this out later). He pleaded with me to come home, just for one night. I reluctantly agreed, but only if he was willing to hear me out and listen to me. He agreed so I went and picked him and his dog up. When we got home I sat us down around the kitchen table where all family discussions were held.

At this stage he had already made his mind up that he wanted to go to Shalom House. We discussed life and what he wanted to do to move forward. He then called Peter but Peter didn't answer. He left him a message and then went to bed. The following morning he called again and was questioned by Peter, if he was ready. Peter asked for him to take a photo and send it through. Jesse sent a photo from a while back. This is not what Peter wanted. Peter wanted to see him as he was now. Peter said he wasn't ready and hung up on my son. My son threw his phone to the other side of the room in despair and started to cry, saying nobody wanted to help him.

It was tough but I said, "If you really want something you need to fight for it."

Over the next few hours, my son called Peter, messaged and called again.

At this stage, I said he needed to go back home as we had only agreed to one night. His dad took him home but the dog stayed. He felt he couldn't look after his dog as well as himself right now. I was so scared for him. I didn't know what he would do but I knew that if he had stayed he wouldn't have done anything but try to convince us to stay here and all that would have done is start the cycle all over again. Then once home he called me in a frantic state that he could go to Shalom House but needed to be there by 5pm. It was now around 3:30. We were in Mandurah. He was in Rockingham so we had to try and get him to Henley Brook in 1 1/2 hours. It was a rush but we got him there.

Fast forward 3 months.........

Unfortunately or fortunately, (however it may be perceived) he lasted two weeks and got into an altercation and felt he couldn't stay anymore. Everyone thought he was doing so well too. There were circumstances around why he lost his cool though and even though he left he has since been diagnosed with something that has plagued him since he was around 10 years of age and it turns out may have been a major contributing factor to why he chose drugs to numb the pain of life.

> ***"If it hadn't been for the amazing work that Shalom House put into my son, I very much doubt we would have had such a happy ending."***

His life has been amazing since this time. He has found God and continues to attend Church and Connect Groups in our area. He even went to a four-day Church Conference funded entirely by himself. He is working again. He is mostly happy but still has a long way to go but is definitely heading in the right direction.

If it hadn't been for the amazing work that Shalom House put into my son, I very much doubt we would have had such a happy ending.

1. How has your family changed through the journey of addiction?

We are very fortunate to have a close family bond. My husband and I have always supported each other with any decisions we have made or rules we have implemented. We have all become very wary though and trusting our son is still very hard to do. I believe I stress more about things that haven't even happened yet.

2. With the chance to do it again, what would you do differently and why?

I hope we won't have to go through anything like this again but if so, we would send him packing at the very first instance we found out he was using or dealing again. We would not be giving him the benefit of the doubt ever again.

3. What did you do that you shouldn't have?

We tidied up the physical mess he left behind 3 times after he had moved out of a house he had been renting. The first two times we shouldn't have but for respect of the poor owners we cleaned the houses up. The last time we did this only because he was going to Shalom House and again we felt sorry for the owner but were hopeful for the future this time.

4. What did you try that worked?

We took the advice to not let him back into the family home. It didn't work at first. It took a good year, maybe more, and he went from bad to worse at first and even had another 8-week stint in jail, as we wouldn't bail him out. One day just before he went to Shalom he called me and asked if he could stay the night, as he felt suicidal. We let him stay one night. This was when he decided he wanted to go to Shalom House.

The following day he kept on calling and texting Peter with no luck. When it seemed he wouldn't get in I said he had to go home as we only agreed to one night and it was now up to him to continue to call Peter but he wasn't staying at home anymore. I know for a fact that if we hadn't taken him back to his house that day he would not have kept on calling and would have tried to stay at home indefinitely. He was at such a low point in his life and it would have been so easy for me to take him back. This is what my maternal instincts were wanting to do but if I did we would have just started the whole cycle again.

5. What did not work?

We let him move into one of our investment properties a few years ago just to get him out of the house, thinking that by giving him responsibility, he would sort himself out. Instead it was the start of major problems of drug abuse and dealing, as well as crime sprees. It was the worst decision we had made, so it turns out.

6. What changes did you see taking place?

After his time at Shalom House, even though it was only for a short time we saw a massive change. His dedication to God was and still is amazing. His attitude towards us was very positive. He also was talking about stuff more and was also able to tell a psychiatrist the true and full story of what he was dealing with in his head since he was around 10 years of age. Had we known how he was feeling and what he was dealing with years ago the problems with our son and drugs may have been a very different story. I still think that he has a long way to go and is still making the occasional silly decision but we are so thankful that Peter gave him a chance.

7. What suggestions do you have for families?

Be persistent with any decisions you make. Take advice from people who have been in the same position. If you find out your son is doing drugs and he is still living at home he has to go, no matter how heart breaking this decision may be. He will NOT try to change his life or get help if he has a comfortable bed to come home to.

8. How did you enable?

By allowing him to come home a few times when we had hope he had stopped his drug use, even after he had been released from jail. It was always only a matter of time before he slipped back in to the life he knew. Each time he started his drug use again it just broke our hearts just that little bit more.

9. How did you look after yourself and other family members?

Just by being there for each other. Allowing each other to vent.

For me, I sought counselling and attended a few workshops that helped me and made me realise it was not my fault. We allowed his brother and sister to talk openly with us about how they felt. My daughter especially felt she couldn't live at home anymore as she felt unsafe during the worst times which I felt very sad about. My older son distanced himself more from any discussion regarding his brother for a while but does now talk more about things.

10. Where did you go for help and what was the outcome?

I attended counselling sessions through ARAFMI which is now called Mental Health Carers, a brilliant lot of counsellors. I also visited my daughter more often and we developed a stronger bond because of all of this.

The following are some answers from other parents who have and are going through challenges with a loved one in addiction.

Carol P

1. How has your family changed through the journey of addiction?

Our family has lost a member, our son, brother and grandson. I know his dad and I carry great sadness and regret within us now. We are still fighting for him but often feel we are losing him or have lost the battle forever.

2. With the chance to do it again, what would you do differently and why?

Knowing what I know now about ice and knowing he started at such a young age I would have tried to intervene at an earlier age and get him to accept help. I don't know if it would have worked but it's possible. I would not have helped him avoid early consequences by rescuing him in times of crisis. I would have researched drugs earlier and tried to get him to see a doctor or counsellor. I would not have helped him financially all the times I did.

3. What did you do that you shouldn't have?

I helped him financially too often by paying his rent, petrol money and food, when he had spent all his money on drugs. I allowed him to stay at our house for too long, knowing he was using drugs but not wanting to kick him out. I bailed him out of jail just the one time, believing him when he said he would go to drug court next time and he would stop using drugs. I paid for him to stay in hotels.

4. What did you try that worked?

Nothing I have tried in the past 4 years has worked. Not one thing, he is still using and still resisting help and still in denial even after jail, drug court, homelessness.

5. What did not work?

Giving him a place to live, giving him money, bailing him out of jail, buying him phones, clothes and food. Begging him to get help. Giving him information on rehabs.

6. What changes did you see taking place?

I have seen him go from bad to worse. He now suffers psychosis and does not seem like the son I once knew. He is so sad all the time. He is homeless. He steals his brother's t-shirts off the line while his brother is at work. He has no family or friends.

7. What suggestions do you have for families?

I cannot suggest as I need suggestions myself.

8. How did you enable?

Financially for the past 4 years if he asks for money I send it. Not large amounts usually, but he can tell me any story what he needs it for and I believe him momentarily until I send it and then I realise he was lying. Bailing him from jail was the stupidest thing I did. He was on relatively minor charges but while on bail he committed further crimes that were more serious.

9. How did you look after yourself and other family members?

I take holidays regularly where I try not to think about it. I began to go to Nar-Anon meetings and that has helped me see that I am powerless over his addiction. I have learnt and am still learning to let go and let God. I support my family members on any decision they make concerning their brother, son, grandson even if it means they charge him for crimes and he gets arrested. It is their right to do so and I support them.

10. Where did you go for help and what was the outcome?

He is yet to get help. I attended one of your information days. I have given him numbers to call for Shalom House (he tells me in the past he has called but I don't know if that's true), Addictions Specialist Doctors (made him an appointment that he didn't keep), most recently given him the number for Wandalgu, after speaking with my pastor who runs Wandalgu, who said he would try to help him and my son said he will call them (I'm waiting to see if he does). His dad and I recently took out private health cover for him with the hopes he may want help soon and could go to the Blackwood River Clinic at Nannup.

Gillian R

My mum is an alcoholic and I remember the day when I was six and I found out. I had no idea what it meant but I knew from that point on my life was going to be bad and it was. To cut a very long story short, my mum has now been sober for six years. :)

1. How has your family changed through the journey of addiction?

Our family has been torn apart, because of addiction. My older sister doesn't speak to either mum or me, so we also have nothing to do with her kids. Which is a very sad situation. The impact of my mum's addiction on all of us is huge and it changed all of us in many different ways.

2. With the chance to do it again, what would you do differently and why?

I wouldn't do anything differently because although there were periods where I didn't speak to my Mum, at the end of the day, I never gave up on her and I've been the only person who has always stood by her.

3. What did you do that you shouldn't have?

I shouldn't have been violent towards my mum but when you grow up in violence and you're so angry, you hit out because you don't know any other way to deal with your anger.

4. What did you try that worked?

Nothing that I did worked... I begged, pleaded, cried my heart out asking her to stop drinking but until she was ready, it was a hopeless case.

5. What did not work?

Pouring out her wine never worked! She would just get in the car drunk as a skunk to get more. Being in her face about her drinking, it was as though it drove her to just do it more.

6. What changes did you see taking place?

My beautiful, loving and caring mother became totally self-absorbed. She became a violent, nasty drunk and everything else came second to her wine. She put us in situations that she never would've dreamed.

7. What suggestions do you have for families?

I would say never give up on them. Yes, tough love is needed and people may need to cut off their loved ones, but never turn your back on them. Always have the door open and don't hold it against them.

8. How did you enable?

I never enabled. When I was older and had my own place if mum wanted to come over, there was a no-booze policy. This is where my sister and I were very different because she would enable by buying, taking mum through the bottle-o and then once she had drunk her 2 bottles and wanted more, all hell was on.

9. How did you look after yourself and other family members?

I pretty much looked after myself. There were six years between my sister and me so as soon as she could get out, she was gone. So for a lot of it, I was there by myself while Mum was blind drunk and getting the shit kicked out of her.

10. Where did you go for help and what was the outcome?

It wasn't till I was older and dealing with my own addictions that I started to go to counsellors, but the very best thing I did was a 4-day retreat and that changed my life. For the first time I wasn't angry anymore and ever since there has been so many changes for the better in me. I walked out of there promising never to touch drugs again. Five years later never have. A while after I had done the retreat and about a year into mum's sobriety, she also did it.

Chris T

I hope this helps. It relates to my son Kaiden (24) who has been a meth addict for eight years now. I have not planned this out, just let it flow. I hope it makes sense.

How has your family changed through the journey of addiction?

The family has been through a lot. We have become wiser, more tolerant, more appreciative and less judgemental. We have lost contact with some friends and some family members as a result of our son's addiction. We know who our true friends are. It is a humbling experience to watch your loved ones struggle and to know that you cannot stop it. We struggle with the sense of helplessness. We grieve for the loss of our son, his life, his hopes, his dreams, the promise he had, even though he has not died. My family love our son and would give away all we have to have him back, free from meth.

1. With the chance to do it again, what would you do differently and why?

I would believe that this was possible. Initially I did not believe my son would use meth and much less become a meth addict. He told me once and I laughed it off 'sure you do'. This denial and closed eyes approach cost me any chance to provide early intervention. It wasn't until I found a crack pipe in his room that it hit me, by then it was too late. At the same time, his behaviour was becoming unmanageable and the demands for money became threats. Rather than continue to offer help and compromise, I forced him to leave my house.

At the time I didn't see any alternative, I still don't but I still regret doing it, I regret having to do it. We have allowed him back several times over the years, each time items get stolen, the aggression returns and I ask him to leave. Every time this happens, a little piece of me dies.

I always replay the incident asking him to leave over and over,

I see the hurt in his eyes, I see the fear and worry in my wife and daughter. We don't want him to go, we want it to go.

2. What did you do that you shouldn't have?

I got angry. I said and did irrational things. Although I never stopped loving him, I did stop trusting, I did let others know what was happening when maybe it was not their business to know. On a few occasions, I took out a restraining order to prevent him returning to the house. People said it was just a piece of paper and meant nothing. It is now one of the reasons my son is in jail. My advice is think very carefully before you take out a VRO as 9 times out of 10, a meth addict will not stay away and this will result in a custodial sentence. In some cases it can be a good thing, but consider whether your loved one will benefit from incarceration. Fortunately my son seems to be thriving in Casuarina prison. I'm hoping to meet my real son when he is released.

3. What did you try that worked?

We did offer to provide assistance in the form of a trip to Fresh Start clinic in Subiaco. Then the planets aligned, he agreed to take naltrexone implants and met George O'Neill himself, who talked with him for an hour. George could see the person inside and offered Kaiden a place in his Fresh Start rehab facility in Northam. I drove him up to Northam that same afternoon. This worked for approximately three months, my son re-emerged and engaged in communal activities. Residential rehab worked well for 3 months until he decided he was cured and against the advice of the staff he left and relapsed within a week. The other thing we have done that has worked is maintained contact and always been there in times of crisis. It would have been all too easy to break off contact during the worst of it; however, we would have lost a son by doing that.

4. What did not work?

Getting angry, blaming him and associating all bad events with him. We tried to impose some basic rules when we let him back into our house. This definitely did not work as an addict will say anything they need to say to get what they want. He agreed to all our rules and then continued on as normal. This caused so many arguments and so much friction. In hindsight, this was naïve, believing that he would live by our rules. I guess the underlying message is don't try to control an addict by imposing rules.

5. What changes did you see taking place?

My beautiful son was the most popular kid in the neighbourhood, handsome, talented and always looking out for the underdog. He made friends with those who needed help more than most. At first I attributed his changing behaviours to typical teenage antics, however it was when he did not respond to typical teenage behaviour modification techniques that we started wondering. He had an marine engineering apprenticeship, a girlfriend and a life of promise ahead of him.

Gradually he became moody, unsociable, started engaging in activities we did not approve of (graffiti, petty theft). The more it happened the more we reacted, the angrier he became. He went from saving money for a car to never having a cent to his name, his pay disappeared the same day it arrived. He became excessively spontaneous, he had to go out and see a friend now, he had to go to the shops now. After a while we cottoned on to all the lies as to where the money went and why he had to go out right now. We began confronting the lies by demanding proof. Rather than cease the lie, it grew, he kept adding to it. He knew that we knew he was lying, but he could not bring himself to admit it. Even when it was laughably obvious that he was lying. He started mixing with dodgy people and bringing them to my house. His good friends walked away and got on with their lives, his new friends stole from him and us.

6. What suggestions do you have for families?

Firstly, believe that it can happen to your family. I guess the biggest piece of advice is decide who you want to protect, yourself and your family or your drug addict. You cannot protect them both. Usually you assist one at the cost to the other. When it comes to the crunch and a tough decision has to be made, remember your addict has made choices that have led them to this point. They are adults and have made adult decisions. It is not your fault. Do not hold back from making a tough decision. Tough decisions are the only ones that get results and make changes. Engage with others in the same boat, you will see you are not alone. Listen to Peter when he says don't stop loving them, just stop supporting their behaviours. Remember if you take away the meth and other drugs, your loved one is still there. If you walk away from both, you will probably lose both. You only want to lose one of them, the drugs.

7. How did you enable?

We enabled out of love, we did it with the best of intentions. One of the hardest parts of having a family member addicted to drugs is watching them struggle and watching them live in squalor. It hurt us to see our family member suffering and our initial reaction was to step in and support him so he didn't have to struggle. This is akin to giving a person with a broken leg a new pair of shoes so they can walk better. Initially we enabled by providing money so he could buy food, we then wised up and adapted our support to only providing food and other items; however this still enabled him to spend his money on drugs, knowing that he would not go hungry as we would provide food.

After a while we had to reduce contact and stop providing this level of support. It hurt us so much as we sat down for dinner every night, knowing that our son was probably not eating that night. Not enabling is the hardest part of this whole battle, it goes against every fibre of parenting we possess. We were aware what we were doing but we justified it. That was wrong.

8. How did you look after yourself and other family members?

We struggled, we argued, we cried, we blamed. Our daughter witnessed many incidents that she should not have had to see. She has seen her parents attacked, she has seen her brother arrested and in jail. She has had her property stolen and has been afraid of the strangers attending our home periodically. She has been the focus of our preventive strategies in relation to our son. Many times we have been ready to allow Kaiden back in the door and she has begged us not to. Many times we were faced with the choice, which child do we protect? My wife and I agreed to disagree many times and often we would switch points of view. We disagreed but we never issued ultimatums or never got personal in our disagreements.

9. Where did you go for help and what was the outcome?

We have been to a range of support agencies, help lines, rehabs and events. The public health system does not help at all with drug addicts, even when they are suicidal at rock bottom, no judgement there, I guess they have seen too much of it. We have sought assistance from the police in times of duress. Ninety percent of the police are great and do their job admirably, but the other 10 percent who do not, do more damage than the other 90 percent can ever undo. Unfortunately I will not call the police anymore unless the matter is life threatening for fear of getting the 10 percent.

We have attended Fresh Start clinic — much respect to George O'Neill and his team who do a fantastic job. Whether you agree with naltrexone or not, they are an avenue of help for so many. The Northam Fresh Start rehab facility is also a fantastic organisation who were a great source of hope and support to my son. Their downfall was that they could not stop my son from walking out or convince him to complete the programme. The peer support was the best thing about his time there.

We have visited a Shalom House event in the Swan Valley and been exposed to the light that is Peter. The outcome of listening to Peter speak was a cleansing of all our disagreements and misconceptions. I've never heard anybody capture it quite like Peter. My goal is if my son relapses when he is released, is to get him to Peter. as I believe that is his only chance.

Michelle C.

1. How has your family changed through the journey of addiction?

My beautiful son became a liar, deceitful and selfish. It changed my family so much, devastated me, my daughter and grandparents. It has honestly left me feeling helpless.

2. With the chance to do it again, what would you do differently and why?

I would listen to that little voice inside of me, as parents we WANT to believe our child, we WANT to not believe they would stand there and barefaced lie to us. I would listen to that voice that said, something is not right here.

3. What did you do that you shouldn't have?

I believed his lies and deception, when in my heart I knew that it was not true.

4. What did you try that worked?

Nothing worked, reasoning, guilting him out. I did not understand the cycle of addiction and what would work. I was not given any constructive advice to help him and save myself and my family.

5. What did not work?

I tried everything, different rehab centres to be told 3-6 month wait, Headspace, local drug centres, nothing worked because addicts become the best liars.

6. What changes did you see taking place?

After three weeks, I saw glimpses of the child I had raised. I got a hug that was a real hug not a quick hug. I saw him clear-eyed but mostly what I have seen is a young man who wants to be proud of himself again and regain self-esteem.

7. What suggestions do you have for families?

Do not give them money, do not believe the lies, if it doesn't feel right it's not right. Do not allow them to use your car under any circumstances.

8. How did you enable?

Let him use my car. I didn't give him money, but I paid all his bills and I still have thousands of bills in my name.

9. How did you look after yourself and other family members?

I didn't, couldn't; so much energy was put into trying to see if he was high. My family suffered so badly.

10. Where did you go for help and what was the outcome?

I tried every rehab (3-6 month wait), Headspace, drug and alcohol centres, counselling. No help by any of these places that actually helped us.

TOUGH LOVE

CHAPTER ~8~

Shalom House Testimonies

BELOW ARE SOME TESTIMONIES FROM FELLAS AT SHALOM

DANIEL SWAIN'S STORY

Hello, my name is Daniel. My story begins in March 1995.

I'm the second-born son. In my case ground zero was Kalamunda District Hospital.

My parents were not perfect, but they did their best for me and my two brothers, Eddy and

Luke, including enrolling us in to private school education for the first few years of our schooling.

When I was around the age of six, I was raped at the park down the road from my family home in Canning Vale. Until I came to Shalom House I hadn't opened up about that subject and I kept it hidden. Even though I was too young to understand what was happening, I knew it wasn't right and I guess that's why the memory stuck around.

I've always been blessed. My mother and father have always wanted the best for me and my brothers, teaching us good fruitful values from day one. Unfortunately somewhere along the way, sin was introduced in to my life.

I became a talented and cunning thief, a deceptive compulsive liar and I would put my hand up to anything bad. To put it simply, I just didn't care.

At age six I was enrolled at Thornlie Christian College, in the Perth suburb of Southern River. It was close enough for my mum to drive my brothers and I to school. I remember dressing up in my older brother's uniform and wearing it to day care. I always looked up to Eddy, as every younger brother would. I wanted to be so much like him.

I always wanted to be around him, often thinking that if I always wanted to be around my older brother, maybe my younger brother Luke always wanted to be around me. It brings a tear to my eye just thinking about the way I treated my younger brother. He never deserved to get flogged or chased with knifes and it never stopped. I've pulled guns on members of my family. I've threatened to kill them. I've stabbed my brothers, thrown knifes at them and chased them with axes and hammers down the street, when I was a kid.

Most of all, I was never a role model for Luke. I often think I'm the reason he never got into drugs, alcohol and crime. He had seen the mess I made of my life when drugs came into the picture. Everything skyrocketed out of proportion most of the time. I was a functioning addict – able to keep my job during the day and go on my crime sprees at night. My garage and bedroom often filled with stolen goods and weapons.

"Methamphetamine and the manufacturing of meth stole years of my life."

Methamphetamine and the manufacturing of meth stole years of my life. That drug was the reason I lost all the respect from my family and friends and through no fault of anyone but myself. My actions and the choices I've made not only resulted in the destruction of my health, both mentally and physically; but also the loss of my happiness, my friends, cars and job opportunities.

The turning point for me came in September 2016. I was continuously showing up to work in a bad state. My untoward lifestyle had come unstuck. I was copping the worst criticism from my work team and I knew I needed to change. I called Pastor Michael Greaves from my childhood church, Victory Life Centre, and arranged to meet with him.

That day I thought to myself, "If there is a God, I need his help, I can't stay the same and I desperately want to change my life."

I remember the meeting at the Victory Life Centre as clear as day. There wasn't any air conditioning in that office, yet I got goose bumps up my arms on a hot summer day. The realisation that I had been smashed to pieces by the Holy Spirit came to me during my time at Shalom House. Since asking God into my life, He has been moulding me and shaping me to be the man I was called to be.

Only now that I'm clean and free from the influence of drugs and alcohol can I look back, coming to the realisation that so many years of my life and countless opportunities have been tossed aside. As I rode the highs and the deepest lows, as I chased the thrills that have resulted in the destruction of many families and lives.

I now have the love and respect back from my family. I am changing more and more with every day that God brings my way.

Fortunately, I didn't kick the bucket and the penny has finally dropped, so I'm going to use my experience as a game changer for the remaining years of my life.

If my testimony can change the choices that even one person makes and better the understanding of the choices they make, then telling my story will be worth it.

STEVE HEMPSELL'S STORY

Hi people, I'm Steve, the 53-year-old resident of "Shalom House" and this is my testimony. It's taken two months and 50 pages of drafts to compile, it's nowhere near finished but this will have to do for now...It must be a phobia.

It's been difficult to write, remembering and analysing some of the most awful parts of my life. Two months of this has been a depressing but maybe also a therapeutic job.

Something else that has taken a lot of time and prayer is reasoning. There are reasons for everything. Some reasons are convincing arguments, others are "cop-outs".

My testimony is the documentation of bad life to Christ, or to good life. A powerful reason for bad life in the first place is environment and genetics both working against you. Here's a reason for bad behaviour, the story of Johnathon Edwards and Max Dukes; the story goes something like this.

Edwards was the judge presiding over a court case against Dukes, the verdict of which doesn't matter to us. Our interest is in the future generations of these two very different men. Edwards spawned a family tree of perhaps 20 generations up to date. In these generations, there is no shortage of doctors, judges, social leaders and healthy, wealthy people. This family has made the American economy mega dollars.

The opposite is true of the Dukes family tree, where unemployment, prison and welfare are the norm, over the same period of time. The Dukes family "cost" America mega dollars.

"The sins of the Father, hey"…I'm not making light of facing the consequences for our choices and actions, but it seems to me we should be putting in work to turn our families around, and break this devilish behaviour before it begins. A stable, loving life should give no reason to become a drug addict.

And since this testimony is about me...the "reasons" I've taken so many drugs over such a long time are no longer relevant and can therefore be buried where they belong. The only issue I have with drugs now is Peter Lyndon-James teaching me how to not disappoint my God or my family by returning like a dog, to eat his vomit.

One more point, I have Parkinson's Disease and may have to stop this discourse if I have a tremor attack. These are brought on by stress and/or stimulation. I can shake uncontrollably for trying to speak publicly, I can shake just as bad for thinking about dinner. So please don't be too concerned if I can't get this job done.

Back to my testimony. Born into middle class Catholicism, I was blessed with knowledge of God and even an acute awareness of His presence...but even so, when I was eight years old, our Dad left us for another family. This affected me much more than I realised over the next couple of decades. It badly damaged the Alfa person in my family, the one I was supposed to learn from, you know, important stuff like "social etiquette", and how to relate to creation.

The destruction of this family also left my Mum, at the time a young woman, with no home, no income, social shame, four kids under 10 and no man to hold her through this.

As for my life, it went on, seemingly oblivious of my existence. I really didn't know what to do with my time. I wanted answers to things I didn't know the questions for.

The authority figures in my life at the time started to warn me of the relatively new scourge of drugs. They sounded great to me, so I researched them, then set about to find them...you beauty, a purpose.

Looking back now, I know Jesus was there, and He must have been calling. What a different life me and my family would have had, if I had just acknowledged Him.

By the age of about 17, there was wine, women and song in abundance. I had such an infatuation with drugs, I spent 90 percent of my time with the "wine".

One day in my 20th year of my life, I was driving to Lancelin to see a mate, when I was suddenly not alone. I was hit for six by God's Spirit. I felt wanted, I felt incredibly wanted.

I stopped the car in the middle of the road (There were heaps less cars on the roads in those days.).

I got out of the car and yelled at the sky that, "I was giving myself to Jesus Christ."

I don't know what brought this encounter on, but in retrospect, I think God, knowing I would have a son within a year, was wanting to show me how to be a Father.

My Lancelin road encounter was soon surpassed by myself and my friends, (but for the life of me, I don't know why). I have had a few encounters with God, become on friendly terms with Him and learned incredible things. But for some ungodly reason, I backslide to the rubbish tip of Egypt again and again. Just like Israel.

I am aware that some people may judge the backsliding by Hebrews and various other places in the Bible. I fear those scriptures, but I trust my Father's love more.

So, "For God, all things are possible." (Mark 10:27)

Then in December 1984, my son Tyron James Hempsell was born from Shiralee Luciel Cook, and this is the best thing I've ever done.

I'd like to blame my rubbish treatment of my young family on any number of things, and I could make a good case, but God would see through it. So I accept responsibility for all my thoughts and actions....God, I'm sorry.

A brief word on how I've been wasting my time all these years.

I was a junkie, I had a love affair with drugs, a chemical romance, any and all drugs were acceptable. Alcohol, speed, acid, e's, marijuana, barbiturates, all the opiates, especially heroin. Us heroin addicts need the drug every day, you can't just do without...you'll be sick, and you don't want that kind of sick. It's not only a necessary substance, it's the "Hero's Game". We shoot for a death rush, all we can tolerate, one grain too much and we die, forever.

What a life, hygiene goes out the window, trust along with it...never again. I won't glorify it by describing the injection of heroin, just know that it grabs you then "nothing else" is pleasurable. Over forty years, I've had many "times out". Often up to a couple of years. But I keep ending up in the same place...with a pick in my arm.

Okay, regroup, this testimony is all over the place, (like my mind) and I'm getting hassled to finish it, so I'll try to put it together quickly, but with order.

From ages 13 to 53, I've (to quote my son) worked hard, earned money, shot it up my arm and ended up on my bum again... later to be given another chance by God, and to do the same thing as before...Nation of Israel again.

> **"I sat on my bed with a fully loaded .357 Magnum revolver in my hands. I sat there for 4½ hours, bringing this big, heavy gun intermittently up to my temple..."**

In my regret, depression and general drug-induced sadness I've often tried suicide. I've looked at different methods: overdose, gun, poison. I got pretty close once after a drug binge that included copious amounts of heroin, speed, Xanax, morphine, alcohol and more. And then the betrayal of a friend. I sat on my bed with a fully loaded .357 Magnum revolver in my hands. I sat there for 4½ hours, bringing this big, heavy gun intermittently up to my temple, pushing the barrel mouth against the skin, putting my finger on the trigger, breathing deeply...then lowering the twelve-inch barrel, 8-chamber beast back down to my lap.

At different times in my life, I've used Russian Roulette as a method of attempted suicide. A big problem with this method is looking at the gun. You see a revolver exposes a fraction of the rim of the cartridge. My subconscious will to live used to look at the gun on its way up to my head, then knowing whether the cartridge was in the death position...only twice did I not look.

There's lots of "tales of woe" around drug use, I've told one or two, out of hundreds. But now it's time to sign off with a good story.

I was living in the South Hedland caravan park, I knew my neighbours well. One morning 4 or 5 people asked me how the party was, and that they thought us Christians didn't drink booze. After much confused discussion, we worked out that they thought I had a party with 7 or 8 drunken revellers yelling, laughing and singing...I was the only human there, with my Bible open, talking and laughing with my Lord.

This sort of thing was normal, before I started backsliding. Anyway, I have to wrap it up...My up and down lifestyle had to end. I rang Pete at Shalom. He let me in with a mild yet long-term smack habit.

After 6 weeks, I went "AWOL" on him. Four months later, I overdosed and was brought back to breathing, etc. by an anti-narcotic injection kept by my drug dealer to stop deaths at his house (well, lessen them anyway).

I rang Pete and asked if I could come back, he graciously said I could. This time, I want to be here and learn. This time I only had drug use, not drug addiction, a habit. This time Jesus told me to go back and be discipled properly.

MATTHEW DICKSON'S STORY

Hey there, how's it going? My name's Matthew Dickson. I've been a resident at Shalom House for 10 weeks now. Before coming into Shalom, I had been a meth addict for close to 12 years. The last of those I had anger issues as well.

Have you ever been that angry that you just can't calm yourself down? I've lived like that for the last 3 years or so. It wasn't the nicest way of living life but I'm getting ahead of myself.

I came from a broken home, my parents split when I was four. My Mum got custody of me and my brother, but my Dad took me and gave me to my Nanna and Grandpa to drive around Australia for a few years. Mum says she looked for me to no avail, I wasn't to be found.

My Nanna was a full-blown Christian, church every couple of days, reading the Bible for hours every morning. Kinda scared me off it, when given the chance by my Dad. I turned my back on the church until I came into Shalom.

I started smoking pot as a kid around 13, like everyone else my age where I grew up in SA. Soon grew out of it until I started working as a tree lopper where I found myself smoking it every day. Just to ease the aches and pains, I told myself.

I got offered a job on the mines through my cousins. Quitting pot cold turkey was easy for me. Worked on the mines for ten years and put 90% of it up my arm. More money meant more drugs. I started smoking meth.

My fiancée, Krystal, used to wake up and think I'd gone out because I wasn't in bed. Then she'd hear a noise and come out and I'd be doing the dishes or something else to clean the house. Went on like that for a while, thought I was smart and that I was fooling her. I was just fooling myself. The first time I stuck a pick in my arm, I had a mate doing me up when my fiancée walked through the door looking straight at me.

The look of disgust and the realisation that I'd probably just scarred her for life rocked me to my core, but then the shot kicked in and oblivion hit me. Five minutes later, trying to explain myself while the rush was upon me. Looking back now, it wasn't the smartest thing I could have done. But then again, I've made a lot of stupid decisions in my lifetime, this was just another in a long line of them.

I spent ten years moving and selling gear, pills, acid, DMT, for so many people. Lost my fiancée and a couple of jobs, always landing a new one. I decided to try and quit on my own when my little brother was getting bad on it as well. After discussions with my Mum and Dad, we decided the smart thing to do would be to go to Broome and visit Dad.

Little did I know an ice epidemic was about to take the town by storm. Literally watching Broome turn from a stoner town into a paranoid, meerkatting ice frenzy of a town within two weeks. The fact that a police taskforce was set up in Broome speaks for itself.

After 2 years of working for the Broome Shire by day and moving gear and collecting for the main suppliers at night, I was well and truly cooked. Getting raided by the coppers isn't fun and getting pulled over every time I left my house and having my car searched two or three times a day gets old quick.

I'd had enough, my decision made, I rang my Mum. If anybody here has ever driven between Broome and Derby, they will know that you can't do a trip without having to stop to let the big bulls cross the road. In the state I was in, I told Mum that I needed to come home, I needed to get away. I told her the next big white bull I see is going through my windscreen as I left Derby for the last time, heading back to Broome.

To be honest, I think I was looking for an easy way out. For the first time ever out of a few dozen trips, I didn't see one bull, or camel, or cow, or even a kangaroo. I didn't even see another car the whole way back. Somebody was watching over me. I made it home safely and started packing my house up and making ready to leave. I was on a plane three days later.

I came back to Perth a broken, shattered person. I didn't know who or what I was anymore. My place in life was gone and I couldn't for the life of me understand how or why I had dropped so low, as to be invisible to everyone. I tried my hardest to give up but I wasn't strong enough. I went to a first step programme in Thornlie. Talking to psychiatrists and doctors was hard when my mind was such a mess.

At night, my mate would pick me up and we would get on and move gear. I moved gear and collected for him for a couple of months living at his house. Worked for his ceiling fixing business when I could.

I moved into another place when his "business" was back on its feet and he wasn't in debt anymore. Three or four days after I moved he was set up and raided by the monarch. Him and the three boys he had with him running for him are now in lockup for a very long time.

"...the meth had done something to my mind... the drugs and my lifestyle twisted my mind so my perception of reality became a hateful, angry, living thing..."

Moved in with my missus at the time, was happy for a while, moving gear, collecting, standing over other dealers. But the meth had done something to my mind, it had been going on for a while now. The drugs and my lifestyle twisted my mind so my perception of reality became a hateful, angry, living thing that was constantly having little digs at my mind.

Breaking up with her for a month led to a downward spiral that had me doing things to people that I can't talk about.

I moved into a house/squat with several other boys and between us, soon had it kitted out with leather furniture, big beds, big flash fridge, plasma in every room. If we wanted something, we put in on a list and that night went and got it. Got raided several times, had to restock the house several times.

Eventually got back with the missus which curbed my going out with the boys a little bit. Eventually got sick of running drugs around, it does get boring especially when your brain is that fried that you can't tell friend from foe.

Eventually losing the plot so much even the boys in the house were scared to live with me, as I was so unpredictable. To cut to the chase, I had nowhere and nothing. I stayed two days with a bloke I had known for four days moving gear for him so I could stay on his couch. When my cousin messaged me saying I could stay with her if I could guarantee being drug free. I agreed and spent two days on her couch eating and sleeping, eating, eating, eating, then sleeping some more.

My cousin Tania woke me up at 11.45am on Thursday, 4th February giving me the phone, it was Pete on the other end. This was actually the second time I had talked to Pete, the first time I had talked to him, I'd organised to meet him at the coffee shop, instead I got on and went out collecting, ignoring his calls and messages.

This time we talked for 15 to 20 minutes and organised for me to come in to meet him. Little did I know I wasn't coming back out. Looking back now, it's the best decision I've ever made.

I have my relationship back with my mother and sister and my two beautiful nieces. My family no longer think of me as a dropkick junkie and I've gained 30 odd kilos, LOL. I haven't lost my temper since being in here, that in itself was unheard of before Shalom.

I've been in Shalom for ten weeks and no longer think of being anywhere else. Shalom is my home now for the next season of my life and I now have 60 new brothers whom I hold closer than my friends I had before coming in. I have Pete and this programme to thank for that. Thanks Pete.

KAJ BULLIARD'S STORY

My earliest memories concern feelings of abandonment and fear. It was 1980 and I was 5 years old. While my brother stayed with my mother, I was put in Bankstown Children's Home, and for a five-year-old boy, it was quite scary. My mother had recently been separated from my father and she couldn't cope with work and two children. I withdrew and became reserved and watched all the other kids, trying to fit in and make friends when possible.

Bankstown Children's Home at bedtime was a madhouse with kids stamping their feet, saying they're not tired, and older kids swinging punches at staff. I watched all this anger and I remember wondering what is it? At that point in time, I had no understanding of what anger and rage was, and it fascinated me.

I understand Mum's reasons for leaving me there. As a father, I've made heaps of mistakes so I can forgive my mother now for all this; however, my experience in the children's home changed me pretty much for life in the following ways:

- I had nothing but contempt for adults and/or authoritative figures. (I made a new family in the children's home, and then I was sent back to my mother, and I was not happy about it).

- I went quiet and everyone would say I had a learning difficulty.

- I had internalised all my anger, despair and fear.

This early part of my life shaped who I am today. I have been told by a therapist that I started blocking out my feelings in order to cope, and I still do the same thing to this day.

My older brother, Carl, was a child prodigy who skipped a year of school, and is now a professor and lectures Medicine at Sydney University. I was always considered second-best or not as successful. I grew up in his shadow pretty much and felt stupid by comparison. I can remember hearing my parents talking to their friends, saying Carl is the smart one, and Kaj is medicated with Ritalin, so he might achieve more.

My parents would take me to child psychologists as I was very different to other children my age. I was drinking all my parents' wine while in primary school. I was not looking for attention while growing up. I enjoyed spending time by myself, and I did well at school. When you are quiet, everyone always assumes the worst, and when you're the youngest child, no-one really listens to you.

As a 15-year-old boy, I had started specialising in getting myself into dangerous and risky situations. I was, in my mind, invincible and I climbed cliffs and mountains in the Hawkesbury and Blue Mountains often without ropes. I also collected poisonous animals, and I often landed in hospital with broken bones or snakebites.

I was spoken to by a doctor about what I was putting my parents through, and he asked me to try and consider what impact my actions had on others. He felt sorry for my parents as they were always expecting me to die or something. It was in my fifteenth year that I organised myself an apprenticeship and left school. I didn't smoke grass like everyone else, because I simply didn't like it.

I went to a party with a couple of good mates and we got bashed by a gang from another suburb. I was so badly beaten that I took three months to heal, and my mates and I started to use needles secretly, as nobody else was. We stopped hanging around everyone else, and we started getting into bad stuff and getting away with far too much. In Sydney, in the early 90's, there were a couple of suburbs that were lawless to an extent. We hung out in all the seediest places and so it was no real surprise for me to try heroin.

My 17th birthday was supposed to be a night out with my mates, but on this day, I learned my father died who had previously rejected all attempts by me to go and live with him in Sweden, so I obviously became upset. I was devastated, plus there were many unresolved issues that I still carry today. I wanted to die, climb a cliff face or cut myself up, anything to distract or block out the horrible sense of despair. I ended up going to Cabramatta and used far too much in an attempt to just die peacefully.

I did overdose and fall on the road but I was revived by the OD van that drives around all day. When I woke up, I instantly went and used again. This was the beginning of a 23-year opiate addiction which I feel I don't need to say much more about.

I moved to Perth at the age of 20, met a girl and got a great job. I had no real problems with hiding my addiction. In fact, I felt smart about it, so I found it fun to go behind my girlfriend's back, or use or hang out with other chicks. This is why I never loved her but when she had my first child, I married her out of obligation. I had a huge problem and this is a sensitive issue. My wife and I were using. I couldn't quit and I was concerned about the unborn child suffering from some serious illness. I kept asking my wife to have an abortion, but she wouldn't.

When my daughter was born, I spent some time holding her, and I just cried. She was perfect in every way. I counted her fingers and toes, checked her eyes, and everything was alright. After six months, my wife fell pregnant again. My habit was worse and I had more pressure from just having one child. My wife was on the drugs and was feeding my daughter formula because her breast milk wasn't safe. I started with the abortion idea again, but she refused.

Both our parents were seriously concerned as we looked like we were half dead, so both sides of the family got together and threatened us by saying they would report us to the Department of Child Protection unless we stopped whatever it was we were taking. My wife had a healthy boy, and I thought it was like winning the lottery or something. A year later, my wife had fallen pregnant again, but she had decided this time to have an abortion, so I took her to a clinic in Midland. The whole process was easily the most disturbing thing I've ever seen or had anything to do with. The emotional impact on my wife was extreme. This moment in time is the cause of a huge amount of shame for me.

After eight years of using behind my wife's back, I ended up overdosing in our bathroom, and my wife kicked me out for good. She dropped me at hospital and drove off. I have spent many years since punishing myself or getting myself in trouble. I've learnt that hitting rock bottom is temporary as it can get worse and it does. In fact, I've felt I've hit rock bottom heaps of times, only to discover a far worse rock bottom. If you don't recognise that as bad as things are right at the time, if you don't make a change, things will continue to get worse.

My thrill-seeking behaviour has of course led to many hospital admissions, and it's a miracle I'm still alive. Since losing my children and family, I have done time in prisons, almost bled to death from rock climbing falls, survived three serious snakebites, but no matter what happens, my rock bottom or the lowest point in my life was losing my family.

When I first came to Shalom House, it was the first time I had been sober for an extended period of time for 23 years. I met Peter at the office and after a short chat, he shaved my head. This of course is routine and a tradition at Shalom House and it helps to keep everyone equal in our little community. I was in withdrawal for a few weeks and after about five weeks, I started getting to sleep at night.

"I was dealing with feelings and emotions that previously remained buried under a blanket of drugs."

I was dealing with feelings and emotions that previously remained buried under a blanket of drugs. I ran away one night then three days later, I was straight back using morphine, but this time with feelings of regret and guilt. I felt like "I'm better than this" and I also had a very strong feeling that if I continue using this time, it won't end well for myself.

Desperate and sorry that I left the programme, I called Peter to ask if I could please go on the waiting list to re-enter the Shalom programme. I was expecting that I would have to beg him and plead my case for weeks, but he said if I come straight in like right now, today, then he would accept me back.

After my short time at Shalom, I have stopped using all medications which is quite an achievement considering that

I've been medicated for bi-polar and anxiety for 20 years. I'm surrendering to God all my shortcomings and this ongoing process both heals and brings joy.

JAY BLAKER'S STORY

Hey, I am Jay and I'm here to share my testimony about how it was when I grew up and what my life was like living in addiction. I had no hope for my life but now I have a whole new life in Jesus. A month and a half ago my life was fuelled with anger, hate, rage, jealousy, regret, shame and so much pain. It was pure evil. It tore me apart living this way with all these feelings. My behaviour and actions impacted, destroyed and tore my whole family apart. I am so ashamed for dragging my two brothers into my world of drugs and crime.

> *"I currently have no contact or relationship with my mother. Her last words to me were, 'You're dead to me.'"*

I feel guilty for putting both my real Mum and my stepmother through hell. I currently have no contact or relationship with my mother.

Her last words to me were, "You're dead to me."

I still remember the pain and tears in her eyes when she came to visit me in prison. Seeing her pain made me want to cry, but with 30 blokes all around me, crying was not an option. I turned around and started a fight with another prisoner to hide my emotions and I pushed my Mum away.

I have two sisters whom I love with all my heart. I lost my temper with one of my sisters while I was really messed up on amphetamines and I hurt her physically. During all this, Mum got in the way trying to break it up and she got hurt accidentally and ended up with a broken rib. My sister became scared of me and to this day, it breaks my heart just to even think that I could do that to someone I love so much. I love you so much, Kala, and I'm sorry. All these actions filled my Dad with so much shame and pain and ripped his heart out thinking how could his son do all that.

I had a sixteen-year addiction to meth and all the other drugs selling them and taking up to $2,000 worth of meth a day.

"I betrayed my best mate, leading them and others to death. I lost all my morals and feelings."

I betrayed my best mate, leading them and others to death. I lost all my morals and feelings. One thing that plays on my mind is watching a mate overdose. I tried to save him after realising he had died. I dragged him over to a park and left after ringing an ambulance. All this so my house wouldn't get raided; you could say I was an animal. But the hardest thing I have to live with is what I put my daughter, Nevaeh, through, letting her see her Dad messed up on drugs.

She deserves so much better, what little girl should have to put her daddy to sleep, holding and rocking me and saying, "It's okay, don't cry Daddy," not knowing what was going on.

I love you so much my baby, life is going to get better now.

Since I've been in Shalom, my life is getting so much better. I've got hope now and for the first time I'm getting a life for myself and my children. I've got a chance to meet my beautiful little girl, Azzarlie, whom I have not seen for three years. I've got my sister Kala back in my life. I'm talking to my Dad and stepmum, all because of God. God has given me the strength to let go of what I've lost and see the joy in what I've got. Also God gives my hope that I'll get my Mum back one day. I'm no longer full of hate, anger, shame and regret. I've got love, hope and joy and I'm just thankful to be alive.

Ephesians 4:22-24 (NLT paraphrase)

"I throw off the old, sinful nature and my former way of life, which is no longer corrupted by lust and deception. Instead I've let the Holy Spirit renew my thoughts and attitudes as I continue to surrender to Jesus as Lord of my life to bring me closer to Him and make me more like Him."

"When I came to belong to Jesus Christ I became a new man, no longer trapped and haunted by the fear of being lost and held down by my old life because a whole new life has begun. And all of this is a gift from God who brought me back to himself through Jesus Christ. And God has given me this opportunity to help others come from the darkness into the light of God."

SIMON HORDER'S STORY

Hi everyone, my name is Simon Horder and I am 36 years old. This is my testimony. I was born in South London, England. I am the youngest of two siblings, with one older sister. My upbringing was a fairly normal one. I came from a stable home,

Dad worked long hours and rotating shifts to provide for his family the best he could. Mum was a full-time stay-at-home mother to myself and my sister. Life was great.

For me, I think things began to change towards the end of primary school when I became a victim of bullying, suffering both mental and physical abuse.

By the time I was in high school, I had become a master of hiding my true feelings, especially from my family and friends. On the outside, I would try to be that happy, normal child that enjoyed school, hanging out with friends and being sociable. But the truth was, my confidence was suffering. I had no self-esteem and felt very insecure.

One of the earliest memories I have of bullying, that still sticks with me to this day, was when I was leaving soccer training after school one afternoon. I was heading home on my pushbike, stopping halfway to cross the road right where a group of older kids were crossing at the same time. Without many words exchanged, they surrounded me so I had nowhere to go, then one of them started punching into me while the rest of them stood back and watched, cheering him on.

I was about 10 years old when this happened. I didn't retaliate or try to fight back, I just remember feeling so scared, helpless and fearful. The cuts and bruises healed a few weeks later, but the feeling of fear never left me. I didn't know it at this stage, but this event and the emotional scar it left on me played a major role in leading me down the destructive path to a 14-year meth addiction.

Moving forward a couple of years in 1992, Dad and Mum decided it was time for a family holiday and brought my sister and myself out to Australia to visit family. We instantly fell in love with the laid-back culture and way of life, that we emigrated here 12 months later. At age 14, I was in Year 9 at Applecross State High School. The move to Australia and starting a new school had both its positives and negatives. It was a fresh start, but this meant making new friends and trying to fit in, all over again.

> ***"My heart was full of bad seeds, there was nothing I liked about myself. I felt totally worthless."***

School never came easy to me. Even when I was putting on the effort, it didn't show in my grades. The one thing I was okay at was woodwork, so halfway into Year 10, I decided to leave school and get an apprenticeship. I managed to get one in Carpentry and Joinery while I was working as a chippy at the Sir Charles Gairdner Hospital. Good things were happening in my life, but I wasn't feeling it on the inside. My heart was full of bad seeds, there was nothing I liked about myself. I felt totally worthless.

When I first began drinking, I thought it was harmless catching up with mates on the weekends, but with an addictive personality, social drinking quickly became excessive binge drinking. This addictive personality landed me in some pretty dangerous situations on countless occasions. It even put a major strain on friendships and it was costing me my relationship. My drinking was so out of control that once I'd started I just couldn't stop. I'd either black out, or get to the point of embarrassing myself or those around me.

There was this one time, my best friend asked me to be his best man at his wedding. I accepted but I got so drunk that I left the wedding and walked out on the newlyweds before they even go to do their speeches. What a good friend I was.

At age 23, I first moved out of home and in with a workmate. This meant I no longer needed to hide the amount of alcohol I was consuming, so in turn it became increasingly worse. At this time, I was also introduced to the "party scene", taking any and all pills I could get my hands on. These instantly made me feel better about myself. I felt happy, loving and so full of energy. It was amazing, something I had so longed for, a sense of belonging.

Not long after this I started using meth, first smoking it a handful of times and eventually ending up with a pick in my arm. I used drugs and alcohol to mask my feelings and insecurities. I was stealing money from my family after I'd spent all my own money. I needed to fund my habit. I was using meth to feel comfortable in uncomfortable situations and family and social gatherings. I was constantly putting myself and others at risk, thinking drink and drug-driving was okay.

Consistently over the next 10 years, due to the lifestyle and my own choices, I got myself into financial strife and I had returned home to live with my parents more times than I can remember. This had a massive impact on Mum and Dad's relationship, the financial strain of having to bail me out time after time, plus the added stress of never knowing where I was or what I was up to for days on end.

In 2007, I was involved in an altercation in a house with a loaded hand gun being pointed in my direction. Being able to leave the house early that morning, I went to work a complete mess. I broke down emotionally and confessed to my boss and my mate what had happened. They sent me home. My Dad was home on that morning. I couldn't hide the state I was in. This is when I first confessed to being trapped in a world that I no longer wanted to be in.

After a long discussion with both Mum and Dad, I contacted Next Step in Fremantle and began weekly counselling sessions. For the first time since using had begun, I was able to admit I had a problem and ask for help. Unfortunately this didn't last long and I eventually fell back in to using. The life of deceitfulness, fuelled by anger, bitterness and selfishness was back. I was always functioning enough to maintain full-time employment, though I had hit 30 years old, I still had nothing but a bed, crappy clothes, an old car and a raging meth addiction.

It came to the point where if I didn't take drastic action, Mum and Dad said they would no longer support me financially and I was no longer able to hold down a job at this stage. My sister had said that if I chose to continue down the path of addiction, she would stop any and all contact that I had with my nephews.

I was finally at the BOTTOM OF THE BOTTOM and had to take more drastic action.

I went to Harry Hunter's, a 12-step program run by the Salvation Army. After three months of clean time, and with the counselling I received, I realised I didn't really know myself at all.

One of the earlier questions I was asked was, "Who are you?"

My answer was brief and simple, "I'm Simon", that's all I had.

I didn't know my likes and dislikes. I was a 35-year-old grown man and I didn't know myself without drugs and alcohol. During my time at Harry's, I started a friendship that quickly developed into a relationship, this in turn lead me to leave the program early, two weeks before my graduation date. Once again my choices would cause me to fall even more.

In March 2016, I was catching up with a friend for lunch, who unbeknownst to me, had done some research on my behalf and come across the Shalom website. Right there and then, I rang Peter Lyndon-James. He was straight to the point, and hit me with a few home truths, telling me what I needed to hear, not what I wanted to hear. Three days later, I came to the House for the first time and met Peter for a coffee. After a brief chat about my beliefs, he called me a fart in the wind.

"I truly believe with all my heart that God brought me to Shalom at just the right time to prepare me for the future."

I've now been in Shalom house for three months and in that time, I have been introduced to God, felt his presence around me and I have surrendered my life to him. Since being born again, and beginning a new chapter in my life, The Christian

Way, I no longer carry shame, guilt or condemnation of my past. I truly believe with all my heart that God brought me to Shalom at just the right time to prepare me for the future.

I'm not sure what the future holds, but I do know one thing. He has a plan and a purpose for my life, and right now is helping me to become a better son, and with a baby on the way soon, to be a loving father myself.

TOUGH LOVE

CHAPTER ~9~

You're Not Just A Fart In The Wind

In closing, people often ask me how I changed my life. Well, the following is a little bit of my story. I am unashamedly a Christian man who does his best to live what He believes, and I acknowledge that I have no right pushing what I believe down your throat, but I do try to communicate what I believe by living it and hope that my actions would speak louder than my words. I have written this book in a way that would be respectful to whomever may read it, regardless of their faith and background.

I know that God is real and I know that He loves you, I know it. You're not just a fart in the wind. When you die, you're either going to heaven or hell, and while you have air in your lungs and blood in your veins, you have a choice where you end up.

I had an encounter with Him where I saw the ground move, I had a light appear in the sky and a whole heap of other stuff that has grasped my attention, as well as changed my life. My testimony which you are about to read was written a long time ago and I felt not to change it. I honestly pray with all my heart that as you read it, you have an open mind and an open heart. I pray that what happened to me, happens to you. When you experience His love, you will never be the same again.

MY TESTIMONY

I grew up in foster homes, children's homes and institutions from the age of nine, having spent most of my early childhood being locked up in an institution or living on the streets. I was first placed in an institution for running away from children's homes, not for committing a crime.

I had been molested as a child, made a ward of the state and spent most of my life committing crime, using drugs and running from myself. My parents split up when I was very young, I am the second oldest of five children. I have spent time in all the prisons in Perth, with my last prison sentence ending in 2001 where I served time in Casuarina and Karnet prisons. From a child, up until the age of 31, I was using all types of drugs with speed or methamphetamines being my drug of choice.

Every time that I was locked up as a child, I used to attend these Christian groups where they came into the prison. I mainly went for the food and to look at the girls who came in. I remember when I was 16 in Riverbank Boys Institution, we had a Christian group called Broken Chain Ministry. Pastor Alan Sheppard came into the prison and they played a video called "The Cross and the Switchblade."

I remember going back to my cell and getting on my knees and calling out, "God, if you can change his life, then you can change mine."

For the first time in my life, I knew in my heart that God was real, His presence fell on me in my cell, I remember the joy that filled my heart and the tears that ran from my cheeks as if it were yesterday.

"Amazing Grace, how sweet the sound that saved a wretch like me".

I used to go around the prison telling everyone about Jesus.

God gave me a scripture back then, it was John 8:32: "You shall know the truth and the truth shall set you free".

However, it was another 15 years before I was to come to know what that scripture really meant to me.

When I was released from Riverbank, I stopped reading my Bible and went straight back to drugs and crime. I have been running from me for most of my life. I have been around Australia seven times trying to change my life but everywhere I went I would end up on drugs, then run again to another place and then it would happen again. So I just kept running.

No matter where I went, the same thing kept on happening.

In my heart, I knew God was real because of what happened to me as a child in my cell in Riverbank. My whole life all I wanted was to be normal. What I mean by normal is living with Mum and Dad, going to one school, going on family holidays and picnics, even playing sports and all the things that people take for granted. Me, I went to 16 different schools and only really ever made Grade 6. I have never played any sports growing up or went on any family holidays. To tell you the truth, I can't even remember living with my family. My whole childhood was crime, drugs and everything that comes with it. Over the course of my life up until the age of 30, I have spent time in all of the jails in Perth and had been doing drugs and crime. In my heart, I knew God was there but I never called out to Him.

In 1999 I was released from Bunbury Regional Prison after serving one year of a three-year sentence. When I was released, I decided to sell drugs full time and it wasn't long before I was selling an average of $40k a day in methamphetamines as well as a large amount of firearms, explosives and other stuff. I awoke one morning after I had just done 16 days straight with no sleep and I had the TRG (Tactical Response Group) come flying through the front and back of my house.

They had bulletproof vests on, shotguns in their hands and they were yelling out, "Get down on the floor, get down on the floor," while the helicopter was flying over the top of my roof.

I was charged with possession of two firearms, intent to sell and supply and a couple of other charges. I was released on bail and went back to doing what I was doing and that was selling and using drugs.

Like I said before, my whole life all I ever wanted to be was normal, I didn't want to be who I was, I didn't want to be doing what I was doing.

I've got this saying: "You can take the prisoner out of prison, but you still have to get the prison out of the prisoner."

Even when you're not in jail, you're in jail, even though I wasn't locked up, I might as well have been. When you get out of prison, you try to hang around normal people, but you feel like a weed. You feel like you don't belong, so you go back to hanging around all those people you can relate to, but the problem is they are all doing what you don't want to do, but you keep doing it anyway.

I remember my oldest son, Peter, was just starting his first ever sports game across the road from where we were staying. It was called grasshopper soccer. The deal was the Dads had to stand still with their legs open while the boy had to kick the ball through his Dad's legs. If the son got it through, then the Dad had to roll around on the ground like a goose to make the kid feel all fluffy. When my son kicked the ball through my legs, I couldn't bring myself to roll around on the ground in front of all them people, so I turned my back on my son and began to walk home. I started to cry. I wanted to do that, I wanted to be normal, it was like a battle in me. I went home and told my wife, Amanda, to go over the road and look after the boy.

After that day, weird stuff started to happen.

Every time I left my house by myself, I would hear this voice in my head saying, "Follow me," then the car in front would tap on the brakes a few times and I would hear the voice again saying "Follow me," so I followed.

I followed the car in front for a bit then I pulled up at a park and I heard this voice in my head saying, "I'm offering you this," and there was a father and his son playing in the park together.

I started sobbing and crying my eyes out in the car.

After a few minutes, I drove off and it happened again, the voice saying, "Follow me," so I followed it again and this time I pulled up next to a brand-new home and I heard the same voice again saying, "I'm offering you this."

I started sobbing and crying my eyes out again in the car. It wasn't that home I was being offered, it was what it represented, A place that I could call home. I have moved every three months of my whole life, from one place to another and all I ever wanted was a place to call home where I didn't have to move.

This happened for nearly a week. Every time I left my home, weird stuff started to happen. I was led all over Perth and someone was offering me everything I ever wanted. I would see a family playing together in a park and I would hear the voice saying, "I'm offering you this," and I would start crying again.

I kept on telling Amanda what was happening when I got home and she thought that I had lost the plot on the drugs.

I went out on my motorbike one day. It was a near new VN1500 cruiser and the same stuff was happening. In those days, I used to be covered in gold rings and chains with a bald head, big beard and heaps of tatts, so I stood out a little. I was 30km Perth side of Lancelin, probably 15km north from a place called Neerabup Roadhouse, following this voice in my head, when all of a sudden, my bike stopped.

I pulled over onto the side of the road to have a look. It was a new bike or near new bike. I had heaps of fuel and as far as I knew there was nothing wrong with it, but I still couldn't get it going. So I decided to hitch back to the roadhouse to ring my wife for help. I crossed the road and put my thumb out and this young couple pulled over. So I got in the back and we drove off.

As we were driving along the road, the young bloke leaned over the back seat and said to me, "Mate, I feel that God wants me to tell you that He loves you and has a plan and purpose for your life."

That was it, I just broke down in the bloke's car there and then, weeping. I asked the couple if they minded pulling over to let me out of the car, so they did. I got out, had a bit more of a cry and then cleaned myself up a bit, as you can imagine what a beard and crying does to a bloke's looks and had a sleep in the bush for half hour.

When I woke up, I went back out on the road and put my thumb out and this flat black F250 tray-back ute stopped. I looked at the driver and he had long black hair in a ponytail with half of his face covered in tatts. Now compared with the other car that I got a lift with, this bloke I felt comfortable with.

We started driving up the road and the guy with the ponytail says to me, "Is that your bike back there?" and I said "Yep".

He said, "Would you like for us to pick it up, as we could stick it on the back?"

I told him that I just wanted to get home. We kept on driving down the road and again out of the blue, he looks at me and says, "Mate, I feel that God wants me to tell you that He loves you and that He has a plan and purpose for your life."

I just started to cry and I think I kept on crying until he dropped me off at the roadhouse. I got out of his car and I was all confused. For a couple of weeks now all this weird stuff was happening, I had been led all over Perth being shown everything that I ever wanted and now I had two people one after the other telling me that God loves me and that He has a plan for me. I didn't want to be me anymore; all I wanted was to be normal.

I went inside the roadhouse and took all of my gold jewellery off and threw it in the bin, I'm talking thousands of dollars' worth. I went outside and rang Amanda from the phone box. I told her that something weird was going down and asked her if she could come and pick me up. She told me that she had to pick the kids up from school, so I went back out onto the road and started to hitch. A car stopped to pick me up and there was an elderly lady driving it, so I hopped in and she drove off.

She did the normal stuff like asked me where I was going so I told her, then after a few minutes of silence and straight out of the blue, she says to me, "I feel that God wants me to tell you that He loves you and that He has a plan and purpose for your life."

Now you can picture what happened next. I just broke down crying. Three people in less than 15km of each other telling me that God loves me and that He has a plan and purpose for my life. The lady drove me all the way home to Bayswater and I think that I cried all the way there.

To speed my story up a bit, I got brought to a point a few days later where I had three police holding me down on a road, they had pepper-sprayed my face and had two sets of handcuffs on my wrists, trying to get my arms together to lock me up. I honestly thought that they were going to kill me if they got me in the van. I was screaming at the top of my lungs. I remember them trying to push me into the van, I had one foot on either side of the paddy wagon door and I was thinking to myself, if they get me in there, then I'm dead.

I remember calling out to God for help, I cried out the Lord's Prayer, well part of it. It was the only part I knew and the next thing I passed out. I woke up the next day in hospital with 13 stitches to my head, a tube in my hand and one in my (you know where). I was confused and scared when I woke up.

Amanda was there and I told her I wanted out of there. I grabbed all the tubes and pulled them out, then just left the hospital and told my wife that we needed to go and book ourselves into a motel. I had to find a place to think.

I went to sleep that night in the motel and woke up at around 3 am in the morning. I had had a dream from God and in my dream, He told me that I would be telling people how He had changed my life. I woke Amanda up and told her the dream and all she said was, "That's nice," and went back to sleep.

In the morning, I told Amanda that I felt that we had to go to church. Now I had never been to a church in my life, so we got all dressed up then left the motel, looking for a church. We drove around all day from one end of Perth City to the next, from one church to another.

I would pull up at a church and I heard this voice in me say, "Not that one," so we went from one church to the next when at about 2 pm as we came into Morley this voice said, "That church."

It was the New Life Church in Morley. I looked at the board and the service was not till 6 pm so we went for a meal and came back at six. The second that I walked into that church I was balling my eyes out.

The pastor was preaching on David and Goliath, I remember the words as if it were yesterday, "How dare that uncircumcised Philistine defy the armies of the living God?"

When the pastor gave the altar call, I went forward to accept Jesus Christ as my Lord and Saviour.

I have been a Christian now for just over 10 years and everything that God showed me, He has given me and even more. After being released from jail in 2001, I went to study at Riverview Bible College where I studied full time for three years, obtaining an advanced Diploma of Theology. While studying at Bible College I decided to start a gardening/lawn mowing business and within three years we had 6 staff and three vehicles turning over more than $500k per annum, just weeding gardens and mowing lawns.

I've been with Amanda for 27 years and we have been married for 22 years. We have two children, Peter aged 21 and Rhyan, aged 17 who both went to Swan Christian College and have only moved schools once and that was due to my son going to high school. I also have a very precious daughter, Tosha-Lena, aged 28.

Having lived the life that I have, I had to go through a long healing process where I had to ask forgiveness from many people that I had hurt in my life, with Amanda being one of them. At the same time, I also had to forgive many people that had hurt me or done stuff to me. Amanda came from a normal home, completed Year 12, was Head Girl in high school and even did her work experience as a police officer. I thank the Lord my God for her every day, to me she is the greatest treasure that God has given me apart from our Lord Jesus Christ.

The growth process in my life as a Christian has been amazing from glory to glory, but at the same time it has been extremely hard as I spend time with God in prayer and His word. He continues to challenge me to raise me up to new heights. Every day is a gift. How can I put it into words my love for Jesus Christ and what He has done in and through me? I know what I have done in my life, I know how many times I have let Him down or disobeyed Him and yet He still loves me, He still helps me. I love Him so much it brings tears to my eyes just thinking about Him. There are so many things He has done in us as a family and so many places He has taken us. Over the last 10 years we have travelled throughout Malaysia, Thailand, Cambodia, China, India and Vietnam. For just on five years, I was a volunteer Chaplain at Acacia Prison two days per week. If I were to list everything He has done and how He did it, we would be writing chapter after chapter.

Back when I was 16 years old in Riverbank, God gave me a scripture, John 8:32 (KJV). It says; "You shall know the truth and the truth shall set you free."

It wasn't until I went to Bible college in 2001 where I learned about it in context, in other words, what's before and what's after.

John 8:31-32 (ESV paraphrase) says: "If you abide in me and my word...you will know the truth and the truth will set you free."

God told me at the beginning of Bible College, "...to abide means to live in, to make your home, just like your body needs food, your spirit needs food."

Every day since I was released from jail in 2001, I start my day with the Lord in prayer and in His word. When I don't want to pray, I still pray. When I don't want to read the word, I read the word. When I don't want to go to church, I still go to church. I honestly believe that it is through keeping the spiritual disciplines that I have, that He has grown and stretched me into who I am today.

It's not about being religious, it's about having a relationship with a living God who loves us and I mean really truly loves us more than we could ever comprehend. It's about being a Christian on an everyday basis. It has been through these spiritual disciplines that He has empowered me to overcome all the battles that I used to face, and still face, such as alcohol, smoking, addictions to drugs, the words of my mouth, the thoughts in my mind, etcetera, even right down to paying my taxes on every cent that I earn and to tithing (giving).

Who I am today is not the person I was three months ago and who I will be in three months from now, will not be the person I am today. I am growing in Christ Jesus my Lord every day and will continue to grow as long as I am in this body. What an awesome God we serve, what a mighty God.

The Bible says in 1 Corinthians 2:9 (NIV paraphrase): "...that no eye has seen, no ear has heard and no mind could conceive what God almighty has prepared for those who love Him for those who have been called."

That's not just for heaven, that is for the here and now that is for today!

If you are reading this, I pray with all my heart and soul that the love, grace and power of our Lord and Saviour Jesus Christ fill you to overflowing so that in all you put your hand to, He will be magnified in and through your life. You are loved by God; He has called you by name.

John 3:16 (ESV): For God so loved the world that He gave His one and only Son, (so) that whoever believes in Him shall not perish but have an everlasting life!

Glossary

Acid
Extremely potent hallucinogenic drug LSD (lysergic acid diethylamide).

ADHD / ADD
Attention Deficit Hyperactivity Disorder / Attention Deficit Disorder.

Amphetamines
Psychostimulant drug.

Angel Trumpets
A plant containing chemicals that can cause euphoria and hallucinations.

ARAFMI (Helping Minds)
Mental Health Services & Carer Support organisation in WA.

Benzodiazepines

Prescription medication that can be accessed illegally to become intoxicated or to help with the 'come down' effects of stimulants such as amphetamines or cocaine.

Cash Converters

Pawn-broking chain.

Cellulitis

Bacterial infection of the skin that occurs most commonly on the lower legs and in areas where the skin is damaged or inflamed.

Cocaine / Coke

A strong stimulant recreational drug, commonly snorted, inhaled or injected into the veins.

Cones

Process of smoking marijuana from a bong.

Denomination

A recognised autonomous branch of the Christian Church.

Detox

Process of getting rid of toxins in the body, accumulated by drug use.

Dexies

A central nervous system stimulant, commonly used to treating attention deficit hyperactivity disorder (ADHD) in children. It is also used to treat a type of sleep disorder (narcolepsy).

DMT

Hallucinogenic drug N,N-dimethyltryptamine, otherwise known by its scientific name 3-[2-(dimethylamino)ethyl] indole.

Ecstasy

Illegal synthetic drug Methylenedioxymethamphetamine, which is both a nervous system stimulant and a hallucinogen.

Euphoria

A feeling or state of intense excitement and happiness.

FIFO

Fly In, Fly Out mine workers.

Fresh Start

A WA drug rehabilitation specialising in naltrexone implants.

Gear

Heroin drug.

Glocks / Magnum revolvers

Pistols.

Hammer

Heroin.

Holyoake

Drug and alcohol counselling and rehabilitation service in Perth.

ISA / intrinsic sympathomimetic activity

The property of a drug that causes activation of adrenergic receptors so as to produce effects similar to stimulation of the sympathetic nervous system.

LSD

Extremely potent hallucinogenic drug LSD (lysergic acid diethylamide).

Marijuana

Cannabis plant intended for use as a psychoactive drug.

Meningitis

When the membranes that surround the brain and spinal cord (meninges) become infected.

Meningococcal septicaemia

Blood poisoning, the most dangerous and deadly type of meningococcal disease.

Methamphetamines / Meth

Also called crystal, chalk, and ice, among other terms, is an extremely addictive stimulant drug that is chemically similar to amphetamine. It takes the form of a white, odourless, bitter-tasting crystalline powder.

MDMA

Methylenedioxymethamphetamine, commonly known as ecstasy (E), is a psychoactive drug used primarily as a recreational drug.

Mescaline

3,4,5-trimethoxyphenethylamine is a naturally occurring psychedelic alkaloid of the phenethylamine class, known for its hallucinogenic effects.

Naltrexone implants

A prescription Naltrexone drug implant that works by blocking the effects of opiate drugs. It does this by binding to opiate receptors in the body which prevents opiate drugs like heroin or oxycodone from causing a person to experience the usual high. In blocking the effectiveness of the drug, naltrexone may help to break the cycle of some illegal drugs.

Opiates OPI

Any drug that is derived from the opium poppy, including morphine, codeine and semi-synthetic drugs such as heroin.

Pick

Needle used for drug injection.

Pipe

Glass pipes commonly used to smoke crystal methamphetamine, crack, cocaine, PCP, opium and other drugs that puts the user into a psychotic out of body state.

Psychosis

A severe mental disorder in which thought and emotions are so impaired that contact is lost with external reality.

Rehabilitation

Drug treatment program or facility.

Ritalin

Central nervous system stimulant that affects chemicals in the brain and nerves that contribute to hyperactivity and impulse control. Ritalin is used to treat Attention Deficit Disorder (ADD), Attention Deficit Hyperactivity Disorder (ADHD), and narcolepsy.

Speed

Part of the amphetamine family of drugs, which also includes ice. Ice is the purest form of the drug followed by base and then speed; however, the potential for dependence (addiction) plus physical and mental problems associated with speed is still high. Speed is also known by a variety of other names including: whizz, go-ee, snow, zip, point, eve, gogo, pure, and gas.

Steroids

Anabolic steroids are synthetic variations of the male sex hormone testosterone. Long-term steroid abuse can act on some of the same brain pathways and chemicals — including dopamine, serotonin, and opioid systems — that are affected by other drugs. This may result in a significant effect on mood and behaviour.

Synthetic cannabis / pot

Designer drugs that are chemically different from the chemicals in cannabis (marijuana) but which are sold with claims that they give the effect of cannabis. Sold for recreational drug use.

Tourette's Syndrome

A common neuropsychiatric disorder with onset in childhood, characterised by multiple motor tics and at least one vocal (phonic) tic.

Trips

A psychedelic experience. A temporary altered state of consciousness induced by the consumption of psychedelic drugs.

Valium

A prescription drug (diazepam) is a benzodiazepine used to treat anxiety disorders, alcohol withdrawal symptoms or muscle spasms.

Wandalgu

Residential program 150 kms from Geraldton, WA.

www.ingramcontent.com/pod-product-compliance
Lightning Source LLC
Chambersburg PA
CBHW050307010526
44107CB00055B/2143